Brian Tracy and Marco Salinas Pre

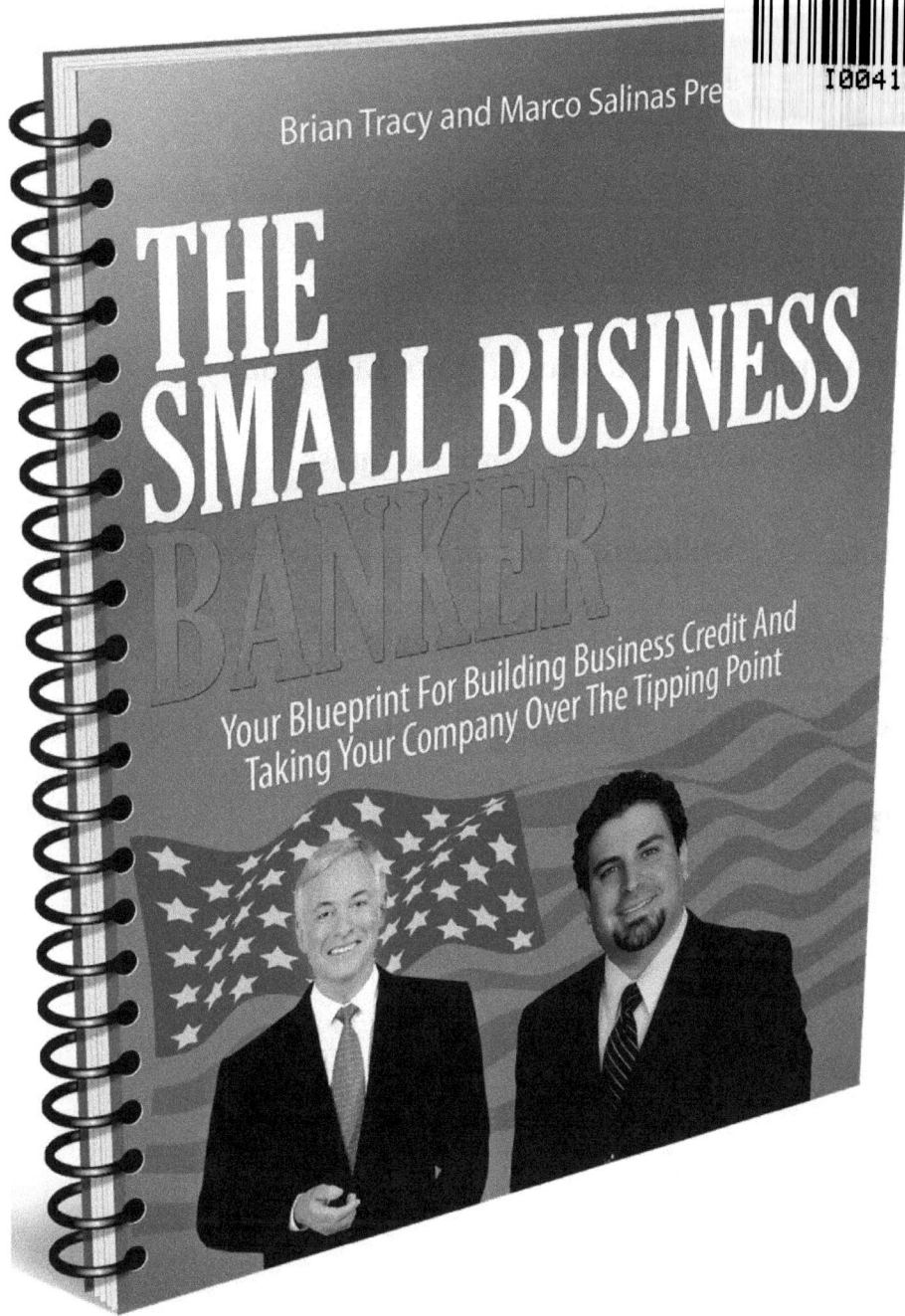

THE SMALL BUSINESS BANKER

Your Blueprint For Building Business Credit And
Taking Your Company Over The Tipping Point

The Small Business Banker

Featuring

Brian Tracy & Marco Salinas

Table of Contents

Module:

Module 1: What A Successful Business Looks Like Today

GREG: Hi, this is Greg Rollett and today I'm joined by a very special guest. We're very privileged to have the legendary Brian Tracy joining us today as we're going to be talking about how your business can really survive and thrive in today's economy.

Brian, over the course of this program we're going to be talking about both your experience in your own business and with businesses that you've been able to help become more successful over the years.

A lot of people know your background as a sales and leadership trainer and they might not see the experience you have in the business world. I'd really love to open up this conversation by talking about the journey that you've had both in your own business and through helping others.

BRIAN: When I started off my career I came from a poor family. I did poorly in school, and my first business was selling soap when I was ten years old, from door to door. I learned something there that changed my life in business forever: I would knock on doors and I would say, "I'm selling soap to go to YMCA camp. Would you like to buy a box?" and they'd say "No. No, thank you; not interested. Don't want it, can't use it, can't afford it."

Then one day, just by accident, and very often businesspeople have an accident and something works and it changes their business. By accident, I said, "I'm Brian Tracy, I'm selling Rosamel beauty soap, but it's strictly for beautiful women," and then I stopped.

All the resistance disappeared. She said, "Well, it wouldn't be for me." I said, "Oh, yes, it would." She said, "Well, then I'll take a box," and she took a box, and I began selling soap like you cannot imagine. I sold more soap than almost all the other kids in the campaign put together.

I sold enough soap for myself and thirteen other kids to go to YMCA camp; I broke every record in the industry. I could sell soap to virtually every single person I spoke to. If I was speaking to a man, I'd say, "It's strictly for handsome men."

It's strictly for beautiful women. My point is this: it is the psychology of the selling. It is the emotional impact; it's the transformation that takes place in the person's life or work that causes a person to buy or not buy your product or service, and if you cannot connect with that, people will say, "Don't want it, don't need it, can't use it. I'm not interested." But if you can connect with that, you can sell your product or service all day long.

GREG: I love that. Throughout this program we're going to talk about how you've transitioned from selling soap to building an international company working with millions of people all around the world and I think that's going to add some great experience and great lessons that business owners can really derive from.

Now, I want to talk about what a successful business looks like. I'm sure it's changed from selling soap to running the company that you guys have now, so in your mind, what are some of the characteristics that make a business successful in today's economy?

BRIAN: If you build a building, you always start with the foundation. And what is the foundation? The purpose of a business is not to make a profit; the purpose of a business is to create and keep a customer. Of all the focus of everyone in the business, 80% has to be on customer creation, and the other 20% has to be on customer keeping: taking such good care of your customers after the sale.

So the purpose of a business is to create and keep a customer; that's the 80%, what we call the point of the spear. The question is: what is the measure of a successful business? The answer is customer satisfaction.

The customer uses the product and is happy that they decided to buy your product or service.

So what is the measure of customer satisfaction? The answer is repeat business. The customer buys it and is so happy they buy it again and tell their friends. Here's the final, ultimate- and this is breakthrough stuff- the ultimate of successful business is that customers recommend you enthusiastically to others and say, "You've got to buy this product or service like I did."

So your customers become your best salespeople, your advocates. The key to all of this, the foundation, is creating a great product or service that makes people happy, that causes them to buy again and causes them to enthusiastically tell their friends, and that has to be the central focal purpose of everything you do in business.

GREG: I think that's really important, and right now I really encourage you to have your Action Guides in front of you. I encourage you to think about your existing products and services and go through them and see the customer experience the entire way through the funnel from the time someone learns about your product to when they buy the product to when they're using the product, because there's different customer experiences for each level of involvement with the product and I think that's really, really important, moving forward in this program.

One thing that I think business owners need to really stop and think about, especially if their business might be struggling in today's economy, they need to stop and really assess where they are in the marketplace, wouldn't you agree?

BRIAN: Yes. One of the most important things that we teach in our programs is what is called "Zero-Based Thinking". Zero-Based Thinking is one of the greatest of all personal and business concepts. It says that you stop on a regular basis, like time-out, stop, and you ask yourself this question: "Is there anything that I am doing today that, knowing what I now know in the current market, I would not start up again today?

Is there any product or service that I'm offering that knowing what I now know, I would bring to the market? Is there any process, any expenditure, any activity in my business that knowing what I now know, I would not start again if I had to do it over? Is there any person that I've hired or I'm working with or working for or partnering with who, knowing what I now know, I would not get involved with again?"

If the answer is no, the next question is, "How do I get out of this and how fast?" Slam on the brakes, because here's the discovery: once the answer comes back "No", the situation is not savable. It's the most amazing thing; you can't go back and adjust it and modify it.

If you say, "No, I would not start this or get into this or hire this person again," it's too late to save it. The only question is: Do you have the courage and do you have the resolution to stop it and start using your time and your resources in better areas?

GREG: I think that's really important to make that stop now and not let it continue as you go. Once we've seen that, we're starting to assess our business and we're answering the questions you just asked. I think the next step, moving forward, is setting real, actionable goals for the business.

I know you have some great theories and strategies and tactics to help business owners set some goals. Once we've kind of looked back and we've answered some questions, we've found some problem areas in our business, how do we set goals moving forward?

BRIAN: There are two ways to set business goals. What most people do is they set sales goals, and your sales goals have to be broken down. First of all you say, "I want to sell this amount in this year," and your business planning, your market planning, your research, is all aimed at giving you realistic numbers of how much you can actually sell.

Everything costs twice as much and takes three times as long in business. Let me repeat: everything costs twice as much and takes three times as long. So if you do really good business planning- conservative, thoughtful, based on research- which most people don't- even then, it's going to cost twice as much and take three times as long, so you have to build that into your calculations.

People say, "I want to sell this much in this year." Well, then they have to break it down to how much they want to sell each month. Then you have to break it down to how much you have to sell each day, and what some people do is break it down into how much you have to sell each hour.

Think of QVC; QVC actually breaks it down to how much they sell each minute. I've been on QVC. There are two ways to be on QVC, and I did not know the right way. So I started talking about my product and how good it was and everything else, and the numbers didn't move.

They jerked me and within 30 minutes I was off of QVC, and I've never been invited back. However, I went onto another television channel later, and I had a morning and an afternoon slot. In the morning slot I did the same thing with QVC; how good my product is and how nice it is and everything else, and the sales were average.

But they had me scheduled for the evening slot, so they gave me one more chance. I went back to my hotel and I turned my whole sales presentation around and I focused it totally on the difference my product will make in your life: how it will improve your life and your work and your health and your happiness and your income and your relationships and everything else.

I went back and I didn't even talk about my product; I just talked about benefit, benefit, benefit, benefit, benefit, and the phones fell off the hook. We sold thousands and thousands of dollars worth of product, and I realized: my God, it's Rosamel beauty soap again! Nobody cares about what your product is; they only care what it does.

So when you start to plan out what you want to sell you have to focus on: what does my product do and how many people can it do that for? Then you have to work out how much it's going to cost you to achieve those sales goals and how much will be left over at the end of the day.

GREG: I think that's really important and I love some of the things you just said in there. I think it, again, goes back to the benefit of what your product can do, and that's really important. It goes back to assessing competition and thinking about your business as a whole, instead of just having the blinders on, thinking, "Well, I make soap."

That's really, really important. What I encourage you guys to do right now is in your Action Guides you have a section where you can start to create your own goals, whether it's sales goals, different numbers, production goals that you want to do, and I encourage you to spend a few minutes going through that because it's really, really important to set these goals.

After you've set these goals, rip that page out of your Action Guide and paste it up right next to your computer or next to the whiteboard near your conference table, wherever you need to see it, because you really need to revisit these things on a regular basis, right?

BRIAN: Right. There's a method that you can use that has made more people rich, in business especially, than any other creative thinking method ever discovered. I use it all the time and it's made me rich. It's very simply called the 20-Idea Method.

Sometimes we call it Mind-Storming, where you actually focus on brining out the best thoughts in your own mind. We do it with groups of business owners, but also we encourage people to do it alone. What you do is you take your goal or problem and you write it in the form of a question at the top of the page.

For example, your goal is to sell x number of dollars worth of product in one year or one month. Then what you do is say, "How can I sell this amount of product by this date?" Very specific question. Then you generate 20 ideas.

You discipline yourself to keep writing until you have at least 20 ideas; sometimes I'll get to 25 or 35. The first time you do this will be very hard, but you keep saying, "I could do this and I could do that and I could do this. I could promote here; I could cut here; I could discount there. I could joint venture with this; I could do strategic alliance here."

You keep writing down every single thing that you could think of to achieve that sales goal, and the most amazing darn thing- and I just did this exercise for myself two days ago on a project that I'm working on- is answer number 20 is often the breakthrough answer that will make you rich, not 19.

People quit after 5 or 6 or 8 or 10 answers because your mind will dry up, but keep pushing, keep squeezing your brain, because you've got the information in there. The 20th answer, and I've seen this for more than 25 years, often transforms people's lives and takes them from rags to riches.

Therefore, 20 ideas. 20 ideas to achieve your sales goals; 20 ideas to achieve your profitability goals. 20 ideas. If you want to have some fun, do it with a group of people and have them throw out ideas.

I worked at a company once- I've got to tell you this great story- their sales were about 20 million a year. Their goal was, over the next two years, to get to 25 million. So I took 17 executives through the Mind-Storming process and we wrote all the answers on flip charts and put them up around the room.

They were skeptical, but they came up with 37 answers; 37 answers to increase their sales by 25 to 50%. Five years later their sales were $104 million. They literally blew the doors off the entire industry, and it was all attributable to the ideas generated in this once session.

Does it work? Yes. The only thing I ask you to do is try it out, and the true measure of how serious you are about succeeding in business is if you hear a good idea, you try it once.

Most people won't try an idea the first time. They've always got to reason. "Oh, I'm too busy, and I don't know if it'll work," and so on. I'm telling you, it works, so give it a try.

Write down your most important business question or problem as a question, and write down 20 answers. Then take action on at least one of those immediately.

GREG: That's a take-action item right now. That might be a pause and come back and visit us in a few minutes. It really does come down to taking action if you want to see the results that you really want to see in your business.

Go ahead; you guys have that exercise and I really want you to take advantage of it because it's worked for Brian, it's worked for your businesses. Just hearing that story; that's really just incredible.

As we grow from that, we've talked about how, with your soap, it was about having the benefits: what's the benefit of the product? That it's only for beautiful women or handsome men or whatever the case is.

Part of that in this economy is a lot of businesses are in the price war, the lowest price war, and that's not the business that we want to be in. We don't want to be seen as a commodity, as a low-price strategy.

I think having the benefits that you were talking about helps you get out of that. How do we transition from the low-price business to getting into get a benefit-driven business where we can get the prices and the affluent customers that are really going to make a difference in our business?

BRIAN: Today it's interesting; the high-price stores, products, and services- Mercedes-Benz, Rolls Royces, Rolex watches- they're selling out of stock. People say you have to cut prices; you only have to cut prices if you can't think of any other reason for people to buy your product or service.

What you're talking about is you talk about the benefit. We talk about what is called a Unique Selling Proposition, a USP, and this is the one reason why people should want to buy your product or service more than any other product or service that's available. You have to be crystal clear about that.

What you do is you offer a benefit that is really, really desirable. Many people say, "This is a great benefit because it'll do this and it'll do that," but the feature is not a benefit. A benefit is a result, and out comes a transformation that will take place in the life or work of the person that is worth paying money for.

What you do is you offer them this benefit. You say, "If you use my product, this is what you'll enjoy. You will become a beautiful woman, a handsome man." People don't care about the means; all they care about is the end.

A good friend of mine has a wonderful way of putting it: if you're selling a vacation, you sell the destination, not the airplane. Most people spend

90% of their time selling the airplane, the travel, the arrangements, the hotel you stay in, the transportation from the hotel, and so on and so forth.

No! People want to know about the warm beaches and the palm trees and the lovely ocean. So you spend 90% of your time talking about the benefit or result that the person will enjoy.

You talk about the pleasure, the difference. People don't buy life insurance; they buy peace of mind. People don't buy investments; they buy long-term security for themselves and your family.

You've got to think: what is the ultimate outcome or result or benefit, and if you buy my product, I promise you, you will get this benefit in spades, and I'll guarantee it. If your product or service is good, people will guarantee it.

You're using an iPad; if you bought that iPad and it didn't work, they would snatch it out of your hand and replace it with a brand-new iPad and an apology, and probably several upgrades and a bonus, and send you a note as well because they take the functionality, the working of their product, the delivery of the promise so seriously, the same as every single successful company whether it's Amazon or Mercedes-Benz or Lexus or anything else. They promise you a benefit that will have an impact on your life, and they stand behind it 100%.

GREG: I think that goes back- and we're hearing some themes recurring over and over again- it also goes back to customer experience when you're driving that benefit and how you're talking about Apple and even Amazon and Mercedes-Benz; it's a total customer experience that goes to the benefit, but it also follows through on that benefit.

BRIAN: Yes. This is something I'm really adamant about; I teach it all the time. I speak to about 250,000 people a year; I speak to thousands of business owners.

Here's something that's so important, and the measure of your success is simply this: how many people, after using your product or service, go, "Jeez! This is a great product! This is a great service!" If they don't say that, then you have to go back to the drawing boards and keep working and increasing the percentage of users who say, "Jeez, this is a great product!"

Have you ever been to a great restaurant and you walk out of that restaurant and you say, "Boy, that was a great restaurant! That was a great dinner! Those are great people"?

Every place that people go back to over and over again, when they describe it to others, they say, "There are really great people there. Great products; great services." The problem, Greg, is too many people are trying to sell average, and sometimes not even average products, by trying to find a gimmick.

They're trying to find a trick, they're trying to find some way to con people into buying a lousy product, a product that they'll only buy once, whereas all successful businesses, going back to my basic model, focus on making their customers so happy in delivering the promise that the customers say, "This is a great product!" and they want to buy it again and they want to bring their friends.

"You've got to come; I'm going to take you to this restaurant." "You've got to see this movie! This movie's incredible; I'll buy you a ticket." That's the kind of experience that you want your customers to have, and if they have that, you can charge almost anything you want and your business will grow and grow and grow.

GREG: I love thatand it makes a whole lot of sense. Again, it's that customer experience. We're hearing recurring themes throughout this first part.

We've really been talking about what makes a business successful in today's economy, and in the last part of this first section I wanted to talk about your team because the team members really make a difference in your business being successful or not, either as a solo entrepreneur or a small-business owner as a small team, the team is really important.

Even in your business where you're out there, you're doing the speaking; you're doing the training; you've developed a team as well that really keeps the machine moving. Can you talk about how you've been able to build a team that you can trust and rely on while you're on the road or you're working with different groups?

BRIAN: First of all, hiring somebody to help you, to back you up, is very similar to getting married. You just don't rush into it; you just don't meet a person and say, "Hey, you look good. Let's get married!" What you do is you have to go slow, and when you start your business, by the way, you're going to make a lot of mistakes.

You're going to have a revolving door. The average turnover for a small business is about 200% a year, and the reason for that is hiring is not only a skill that takes a lot of experience, but also there are a lot of people out there who have only one skill, and that's interviewing well for a job.

So they'll seem nice and cheerful and friendly and they'll have a nice curriculum vitæ of their skills and so on. Within 24 to 48 hours you'll realize this person can't find their bum with both hands. So we see this all the time, so this is one of the things I recommend: we're always hiring.

We have about 15, 16 people and we have low turnover; about 10 or 12 of the people have been there 5 or 10 years, but we do have new people. One of the things I teach is called the law of three.

The law of three in this says interview a person that you like at least three times, then interview that person in three places and have that person interviewed by three other people.

If you take the law of three, what I say is interview at least three people for the job and pick one you like, interview that person at least three times, interview them in three places; don't sit in your same office, same chair. Take them across the street to McDonald's and buy them a cup of coffee.

I once was interviewed by a very wealthy man worth $800 million, and I didn't even know it was an interview. He invited me to come out with him to his ranch; he had a ranch outside of town. We just walked around and he showed me his cattle and he showed me other things.

We walked around and I commented and he asked me little questions about my background and so on and so forth. Afterwards we came back to the house and he said, "Okay, the job is yours." I didn't even realize that was a job interview.

He was just checking to see how I would behave and how I treated other people at the ranch and whether I opened the gate and things like that. He was just kind of watching. I've been interviewed like this before by senior people; they take you for a walk and just talk about general things.

So interview them three times. Now, here's the key: before you hire anybody, have that person interviewed by at least three people other than yourself. You say, "I'm a little person. I don't have a big business." Well, have your wife interview.

Everybody has to be interviewed by my wife, by the way, because women have tremendous sense for whether a person will work out right or wrong. Have your friend who works in your other business interview this person.

Have your accountant interview this person. Have somebody else; three people. Never trust your own judgment to hire when you're a business builder because you're emotional, you're impetuous, you're busy, you're distracted.

You look upon hiring as something you've just got to get over with. Have three other people talk to the person, and then say, "What do you think?" If the consensus is 100%, hire them. If one person says no, don't hire them.

Remember, it's easier not to hire a person than to hire a person and have to wrestle and fight with them and then get rid of them and then get sued by them and all the darn things that can happen to you. Hire slow; we say "Hire slow, fire fast".

GREG: It's a good motto to work with. Building on that, now that you've gone through this hiring process, let's talk about how beneficial your team is to your business.

BRIAN: I have a team, as I say, of about 15 people. Each one of them, as a matter of fact, has been hired through this process; they all know how to use this process, so they actually hire the people under them.

There are about four or five people in my office who do hiring, which is an interesting point, by the way. In any company there are three or four people who have the capacity to hire a person.

That's one of the things, if you can avoid it, by all means do it: when my people hire somebody, I'm the last person to pass judgment. They introduce the person to me after they've been vetted three times at three places by three people.

So now you have a person in place. Then the most important word for business success is clarity. Clarity: each person must know exactly what it is that you want them to do and exactly why you want them to do it.

If you can give them a clear 'why', they'll be very creative in the 'what' and the 'how'. Then what you do is you keep giving and delegating tasks to people that free you up to do the things that pay even more. You always use another factor we call 'hourly rate', and you say, "Calculate your desired hourly rate."

If you want to earn $50,000 a year your desired hourly rate is $25. If you want to earn $100,000 a year your desired hourly rate is $50; that's your annual income divided by 2,000 hours, the average number of hours an entrepreneur works.

Then you say, "All right, I want to earn $25 an hour, so that means I cannot do $10 an hour work. I can't do typing; I can't do checking email; I can't read the paper or make coffee or photocopies."

What you do is as soon as you determine this is what you want to earn, then what you do is you hire anyone else who can do that at a lower hourly rate than you desire to free up your time for doing things that only you can do.

GREG: That's really, really powerful. I like that strategy a lot. What I want to do now is I want to bring this first section and really wrap it up. We've been talking about what really makes a successful business in today's economy.

We've heard some really great recurring themes: it's the customer experience, it's the benefit your product brings to the marketplace, it's about hiring great people that are going to make an impact and free you up to do the things that are going to allow you to grow your business.

Let's talk to the business owners that might be struggling a little bit that are going through this program. What is the first thing, first action, that you would tell them to do to really take that direction to go from where they are now to where they want to go?

BRIAN: First of all, realize that all business owners are struggling. I'm a business owner; I'm struggling. One of the things that I learned many years ago, which is one of the great business concepts, is called the strategic business unit concept.

That's where you take the products and services that you have and divide them into specific units. For example, we have several seminars that we offer; we have several programs and seminars that we give; we have a series of products that we sell online.

What we do is we look upon each of them almost like a separate mini-business; like a separate strategic business unit. Then we have a mini business plan for each one rather than having them all together and everybody's doing a little bit of this and a little bit of that.

You think through zero-based thinking; if you were not now offering this product, would you bring it to the market? If the answer ever pops up 'no', then discontinue it. Perhaps the most important quality for business success in the 21st century, according to the Manager Institute, is flexibility.

Flexibility; be flexible. Realize that almost every decision you make will turn out to be wrong in the fullness of time, 70% or more; every product or service or marketing or advertising decision.

It may be right when you initiate, but that's questionable; but it'll turn out to be wrong because the market will change, so be flexible. Be willing to abandon things that aren't working.

The only questions you ask are: Does it work? Is it working? *Wall Street Journal* today said the most important thing an entrepreneur does is realize that if the customer is not buying it, stop selling it. Don't beat your head against the wall just so it feels good when you stop.

Peter Drucker once said the greatest problem in business is managerial ego. We bring our product to the market, we invest our egos in it, we invest our time, our heart, we tell everybody it is and how wonderful it is, but like the story about the dog food, the dogs don't like it.

If customers don't like it, they don't want to buy it, they argue with you about price, they bring it back, move on to something else. What's the most successful high-tech company in the world today? It's Apple.

Do you remember Apple's NeXT Computer? Do you remember its tablet computer? They brought it out, it seemed like a good idea at the time, it bombed in the market; they just pulled it off the market and moved on.

You don't see them trying to keep on selling something that customers don't like. So be really flexible, be adaptable, adjust to the realities of the market, and be willing to try something new. Try to make your product faster, better, easier to use, cheaper; try different forms of advertising.

The most important thing that you need to know is if you could narrow it down and say to your customer, "You'll only get one benefit: this is the primary benefit." Let me rephrase it: "You'll get many others, but this is the one benefit, more than anything else, that you will get if you use my product or service."

Can you be absolutely crystal clear about that benefit, and then can you guarantee that your customer will get that benefit? If you can't be clear about the benefit, you need to be clear. If you can't guarantee it, take the product off the market.

I work with one of the biggest MLM companies in the world. They're very successful; very high-quality products. Every year they take product off the market because exhaustive research shows that the product is good, but it's not the best, so they just take it off the market and they discontinue it.

People say, "But I like that product! I like that product," including myself. People say, "Yes, but it doesn't meet our standards of being really excellent, so we've decided to discontinue it and focus only on those things that we can quite confidently say are really excellent."

A critical point is Aristotle said that the ultimate aim of all of human activity is to be happy. Happiness is the one thing that we all strive for. The only question is how good we are at achieving our own happiness.

Even Ayn Rand said this in her philosophy of Objectivism. Your job is to make your customers happy, and the whole focus is "How can I make my customers happy? How can I make them happier than my competitors? How can I make them so happy that they buy from me and buy it again and tell their friends?"

So whenever you're having challenges in the market, and there are always sales challenges, revenue challenges, pull back and say, "Wait a minute. For me to be successful, I've got to make people happy."

I'll give you a great story: Jim Collins' bestselling book *Good to Great* examined over 1,100 businesses and isolated several businesses that had been good for a long time and then became great businesses.

One of them was a company that realized- this was a Fortune 500 company, multi-billion dollar company- that the competition was so tough in their industry that they could never be the best in their industry, and by the best it means that you want to be in the top 10% of your industry.

They could never be the best, so they took a great big deep breath and they decided to sell off their company; sell off the factories and sell off the distribution facilities and sell off the manufacturing and sell off everything and take the money and invest it in a new business where they could be the best in the industry, and they did.

Everybody said, "You must be crazy!" Their stock took a terrible beating in the stock market. Today it's one of the most respected, most profitable companies in the world because they had the courage to recognize that we cannot be excellent in this area; we can only be a "me too" product.

If you're a "me too" product, you have to sell solely by lowing your price and by gimmicks and by making claims that aren't true, and then by dodging customer phone calls and everything else. But if the product is great, people will line up.

Somebody said to me the other day, "My product is so good there's no competition." I said, "That's really incredible." This is a business owner, and I said, "That's really incredible. So, there must be a lineup of people around the block every morning when you get to work waiting for your services because they're so good," and he went, "Huh?"

I said, "There's no lineup? Well, that means that your product is not the best product. It's not the irreplaceable product. Your product's available; look in the Yellow Pages. Your product's available from 50 other companies."

He wrote back to me and he said that was the biggest shock of his life. He's been walking around telling everybody that his product is so unique and good it's the best in the business, and he realized that if it was the best in the business his phone would be falling off the hook; his waiting room would be jammed.

People would be lined up in the streets. The parking lot would be full. People would be throwing checks at him over the heads of other people if his product was that good. So don't fool yourself.

GREG: Right. Don't let the ego get in the way; be flexible. Brian's just shared with you some great wisdom, tips, and strategies of what a successful business looks like in today's economy, and I encourage you to go back and go through your Action Guide.

Look at all the things that you can do with your own products and services and with your team to make your products great, to make your customer experience a great place from the time that they learn about your product to the time they buy it to the time that they use it.

When we come back here in part two we're going to be talking about building your brand and your brand both as a business owner and through your business. Thanks again for listening to part one and we'll see you again in part two.

Module 2: Marketing And Branding Your Business

GREG: I am back with the legendary Brian Tracy, and we've been talking about your business and what your business needs to look like in today's new economy.

In this section we're going to talk about media marketing and PR, and then we're going to get into a little bit of branding. These are some really critical elements in order to take your business from where it is now to where you want it to be going.

You know, Brian, throughout your career you've been a front man in sales and selling your own business and helping other businesses with sales and marketing. I really want to kick this off with maybe some fun stories of some successes you've had in selling and in marketing that really have helped your company and your career take some leaps.

BRIAN: Yes. Well, the critical thing is to find out what is the most pressing need or desire of your customer, and then offer to satisfy that need. We say that a good prospect has a need that is not satisfied and they have this need now. In other words, they're hungry.

Sometimes you drive along the highway and they have a great big billboard that'll say, "Hungry?" and they're not looking for someone who's thinking about being hungry; they're looking for someone who's hungry now. Then it'll say, "Turn off at the next exit."

The second thing is that they have a problem unsolved, and the problem is a real concern to them. Third of all they have a goal that has not been achieved, and they want to achieve that goal. Financial independence: the most popular single ad with regard to money is "Lower your taxes."

Everybody wants to reduce your taxes because they consider that money to be literally lost money, and everybody is concerned that they're paying too much and that other people are paying too little. So if we ask a question "Lower your taxes?" it immediately catches people's eye.

The fourth thing is that they have a pain that has not been taken away. The critical thing is immediacy; you're not looking for people to bring in and talk to and convince that they have a need or a problem that your product will solve.

You're looking for people who have it already and are looking for a solution. For example, if you're selling indigestion problems, you say, "Indigestion? Take this!" "Headache? Take that!" "Thirsty? Take one of these!"

In other words, it's very important that you know exactly the most important thing your product or service can do for the customer. Then you find: where are the customers for whom my product or service can do this? Where can they be found?

GREG: I think that's a great place to start. As we build out in this section, we're going to be talking about media marketing and PR. I want to start with media because I think that's the thing that's, for a lot of people, at the front of their mind.

That could be TV; that could be big print; that could be getting in big, major blogs and media. Talk a little bit about how to get into some of those medias, and also: how can that benefit your business?

BRIAN: Okay. Remember, there are 30 million businesses out there right now. Every one of them is fighting desperately to get exposure; you mentioned earlier the importance. The most valuable and most rare commodity in America today is attention, is to get people's attention and hold it.

So therefore, trying to get media exposure is very tough. The average person is exposed to about five thousand commercial messages per day;

in newspaper, television, radio, Internet, spam, wherever they go, magazines, there are commercial messages.

The average person has to just blot them all out. To get their attention you've got to be sure your message is getting through. Let me just start off with what I teach to my business owners. There are four parts of marketing strategy that you need to think about.

What is that most valuable work you do in your business? It's thinking clearly. You think clearly with tools. The first tool is called specialization. What is it that you specialize in?

You can specialize in a product or service, you can specialize in a market, a particular type of customer, or you can specialize in a location. A 7-11 specializes in a location. So what do you specialize in? What is your area of specialization?

You never say, "We do everything." A dentist does not do hair and does not paint toenails. A dentist specializes in teeth, and a cosmetic dentist specializes in how pretty your mouth looks.

You've got to be clear about your area of specialty so that a child could tell another child what you do; what it is that you offer. The second key to marketing strategy is differentiation.

Basically, 80% of all marketing is differentiating yourself from your competitors. It's showing your customers that your product or service is better, faster, cheaper, more popular, useable, more convenient; it will make you happier than any other product that's available in the market today in your price category.

A great example is McDonald's. Nobody compares McDonald's with Morton's but in McDonald's price category, which is inexpensive, it focuses on value, quality, price, and cleanliness. In other words, you get good value, you get good quality, you get reasonable prices, and it's clean.

Also, the people are chipper, the facility is nice, so people know they can go to McDonald's and consistently get that quality of experience, and they sell a billion a year in 42,000 outlets. They're the most successful restaurant operation in the history of man on Earth, but at their level.

Therefore, you have to be excellent within your niche. Differentiation; you have to be different. Better, superior, faster, easier, more convenient in three ways in order to compete in today's market. It used to be you had to have one great area of differentiation.

Today it's got to be three, and you have to figure out what those three are. Those are the high ground, and you've got to take the high ground and hold that high ground against your competitors. Don't allow yourself to say, "Oh, we're better in all these areas."

The only time you know is when your customers tell you that you're better. The third area has to do with segmentation, which is: you segment your market and you say, "Where are the customers who most want what I specialize in and who most appreciate and will pay for my area of differentiation?"

You don't advertise Mercedes-Benz in the ghettos and you don't advertise McDonald's in the upper level neighborhoods. Where are the customers? They say today that all marketing today is segmented marketing; finding your segment.

Then the fourth part is concentration. You advertise, promote, concentrate on the media, the market, the publicity, whatever it is that most reaches the people that you have decided are the very best people who will buy the fastest and pay the most for your product.

So that's strategy, and you have to think it through. Specialization, differentiation, segmentation, and concentration: if you miss in any one of those, you go broke. These are not casual things; if you miss, you go broke, and 80% of businesses eventually go broke because they don't have answers to those four.

The other thing that is so important is what we call the marketing mix. The marketing mix has seven key parts. The first part is the product or service itself and why it's good and who it's good for.

The second is the price; how much do you charge? You can take a price and charge from $9.95 to $10.05, and your sales will drop 50%. Why? It's because up to $9.95 people will pay it; it's called the no-brainer price.

Once you go over ten dollars, it's "Let me think about it for awhile, and think about it forever." So pricing is really, really important. The third part has to do with promotion. What raise are you going to get the goods out of the woods, get the news to your customers, that the product is available?

I'll give you a very interesting example, a radical theory. A friend of mine opened a first-class restaurant, and rather then spending tens of thousands of dollars advertising this restaurant in a competitive market, what he did is he went down to Yellow Cab in a busy city.

He went down to Yellow Cab and he said, "I'd like to invite your drivers and their wives to come to our restaurant for dinner at no charge, as our guests, next week," just the week prior to opening. Restaurants go through a shakedown phase where they test everything out.

So they gave out these awards to the drivers and their wives, and for the next three or four days the restaurant was full because these were time-limited; full of taxi drivers and their wives. They treated them well and gave them beautiful food and wine and everything was paid for.

And what do you think happened? Every single time a businessperson got into a taxicab and said, "Do you know of a good restaurant to eat at?" they said, "Yeah, this restaurant."

The parking lot was jammed with taxis dropping off businesspeople in twos and foursomes. The restaurant was full for five years because those businesspeople then went out and said, "Geez, I went to a good restaurant last night."

So they put all of their money into free, at the beginning, into the minds and hearts of people who would tell everybody else about it. Great marketing strategy, because that turned out to be cheaper than buying advertising.

The way that you promote your product is really the key. We call this the jelly in the jelly donut. The fourth part has to do with place: where do you sell? There are three others. The three others are packaging: what does your product or service or place of business look like?

You'll find, for example, if you take an Apple product, they are insane about the beauty of the product. As you know, Steve Jobs was insane about making it beautiful, making it thin, making it elegant, so that people held it with pride and handed it to people and people touched it, and they sell them by the tens of millions.

Therefore, how beautiful is your product? It must be as beautiful as or more beautiful than your competitors, or you back to the drawing boards. You should put your packages through this test: ask a kid: "Which one would you pick?"

The kid will always pick the one that looks the most attractive. If you don't pass the kid test, you can go out of business; you can go broke. The sixth part of the marketing mix is people.

The people are the people who actually interact with the customers, and they'd better be really nice, pleasant, polite, cheerful people. Even people behind the counter at McDonald's are trained to be cheerful.

The last of the seven is positioning, which we'll talk about when we come to branding; how you position yourself in your market and the hearts and minds of your customer is really the critical factor in whether or not you become successful.

GREG: That's really great. I really love all seven of those keys right there in the marketing mix. What I want you to do is I want you to think about how your products and services fit into each of those seven elements.

Go through that in your Action Guide right now, because that's really going to set the tone as you move forward and you create strategies to now go out and market and get the customer. So let's expand on that.

BRIAN: One point: one small change in the marketing mix can transform your business. One change, if it's the right change and the right time, can transform your business; can take you literally from average to extraordinary if it's the right change. So you keep looking as to "How could we improve in one or more of these areas?"

GREG: I like that. Now that we've really thought about these seven areas in the marketing mix, where do we go from there?

BRIAN: You go and you say, "All right, who, where, and what are the media that are already selling to my potential customers?" I often say to my business audience, "What is the sound that the owl makes in the deep woods?" Everybody thinks about it for awhile and then they go, "Whooo? Who?"

Yes. Last year they spent eight billion dollars on market research in the United States alone, asking the question, "Who? Who? Who is my perfect customer? Who is my ideal customer? What is his or her age, occupation, income, educational background, level of family formation, the demographics?

What are his or her psychographics? What are their fears and needs and desires and wants and hopes and aspirations? What moves them emotionally and spiritually and mentally? What's going on in their minds?"

You have to know the answer to the question "Who?" 80% of new products fail each year because they get the 'who' wrong or they don't even think about it. They think, "This is a good product; I think it's a good product. People will buy it."

No; you should be able to tell me, if I were to ask you, "I know a lot of people in this community, Greg. Tell me the kind of people who buy your product or service. Tell me all about them, but don't mention your product or service. I don't want to hear that.

I don't want to hear the name of your company or your product or service; I just want you to describe the person. Who is the person, ideally- what they call the avatar- the person who would be most ideal to buy your product or service immediately and pay a good price for it?"

If you can't do that, then you have to go back to the drawing boards and do it. Most people start off saying, "I'm looking for someone who wants to buy life insurance or who wants to be fitter and healthier and have more energy and everything else."

No; don't talk to me about your product or service because nobody cares what it is; they only care what it does to transform their life in a positive way. So who are these people? Who? Who, and who are they, and then where are they, and why do they buy, and what value do they seek?

Then what are they looking for and what else do they buy, and who are their competitors and why don't they buy, and how could you offset that? The greater clarity you have with regard to your customer, the easier it is to pick media.

Then you find media that are selling effectively to the kind of people that would buy from you. One of the things that we do, you and I do this, and we do this with a lot of other companies, is called joint ventures or strategic alliances; you've heard about other people's money, other people's ideas.

The great breakthrough in small business today is other people's customers, OPC; you find somebody who is already selling to the perfect customer for you and you go to them and say, "Look, let's do a deal.

Let me sell my products to your customers, non-competing, and I'll share them with you, and then I'll sell your products to my customers. Let's share customers.

They're all the same type of customers; rather than trying to find new customers, the hardest and most expensive thing in the world today, let's go out and sell to each others' customers."

GREG: Yeah, and make it a win-win for both of us.

BRIAN: Make it win-win; share the revenues.

GREG: Exactly. Now I really want to dig onto something because you hit it on the head when you were talking about people and knowing who your customers are, but also in today's landscape- and this kind of segues into branding- people really do buy from people in today's age.

You mentioned Apple, who we mention a lot; we really can relate to Steve Jobs. We love the products, but we can relate to Steve Jobs. Let's talk about the concept of people buying from people in today's marketplace.

BRIAN: This is very important, but it depends upon your product. People say, and I've taught this for years, is when you are face-to-face with a prospective customer, yes, they buy depending on how they feel about you.

Sometimes I'll ask my audiences, "What percentage of customers' decision-making is emotional? What percentage is logical?" After they say 80/20 or 90/10, I'll say, "No, it's 100% emotional."

When you're dealing directly with another person, the make their decision emotionally and then justify logically. The number one reason that people buy a product or service from a person is because they like the person. I call this relationship selling.

If you're selling your products face-to-face, whether it's in a retail setting or it's direct sales, knocking on doors, talking to people, trade shows, where they're dealing with you, it's how they feel about you. If I like you, and I trust you, and I feel comfortable with you, then I will buy from you, because I will assume that you'll take care of me.

However, if you're selling via Internet- and the Internet is transforming all of marketing- even if you're selling via Internet or via newspapers or direct mail or even radio or newspaper, then it's not the person that's selling; it comes back to the benefit that you're offering.

Once you get people, if you say, for example, "Would you like to save 50% on your taxes this year with a new rule that the IRS has just issued and your accountant doesn't even know about, call this number," that's going to get a lot of people phoning the number.

Then you have to make sure that the person who answers the phone is a really nice person, because the one characteristic of people replying to ads is they are suspicious, because they're afraid that they're going to be hard-sold and up-sold and cross-sold and down-sold.

So make sure the person on the phone is really a nice person and asks really good questions about how they can help this person who called in so the person lets down their guard and relaxes and starts to feel good about who they're talking to. Wherever it's people-to-people selling, then the people doing the selling have got to be genuinely nice people.

GREG: I like that, and some of that's going to go back to the business and the brand and the culture that the business has started. Let's really start to talk about a brand.

So we've gone out, we're going some selling and some marketing, we're getting some data back, we're seeing how people relate to our products and how they buy our products. How does a brand play into that?

I know we were talking earlier: you can't start with a brand; you kind of have to start with your customers and your product and your services, and then you kind of build into that brand.

BRIAN: This is something I know exhaustively; I've taught it for years. Theodore Levitt, who is the dean of Harvard Business School, wrote a book some years ago, a tremendous book. It's called *The Marketing Imagination*, and in that he talked about the most valuable asset that your company has, and it is your reputation with its customers.

Your reputation consists of how you are known to your customers, how your customers think about you when you're not there, how your customers talk about you, how your customers visualize you, how your customers feel when your name is mentioned.

What is the reputation that you have with your customers? That is the most valuable asset you have. Interestingly enough, there's a coffee brand in Hawai'i called Kona Coffee. It's the most popular brand in Hawai'i.

It's interesting; the guys who started this company, entrepreneurs, came up and they decided they wanted to do a leap forward by buying a brand that nobody was taking advantage of.

They stopped selling Kona Coffee 90 years ago, but it was still so famous in Hawai'i they paid $300,000 to buy the name Kona from the ancestors of the people who had built the original coffee company in the last century.

GREG: Wow, that's a strong brand.

BRIAN: Then they took that name and they put it all over everything. Within two years, they're the best-selling coffee in the islands and they sell all over the world because the brand, even though it had not been used for 90 years, was still in the minds and hearts of people; they identified with it.

Black & Decker was sold recently to another major company. They paid $100 million for the company: $10 million for the assets, $90 million dollars for the name Black & Decker because it had such a great name.

So how do you develop this reputation? The question is, you have to ask, "How do we want people to think about us after they've dealt with us? When a person walks away from us, if we were going to interview them, what would we want them to say?

Would we want them to say that our products were excellent, that the service was wonderful, the people were cheerful, the building was efficient? Do we want them to say the packaging was great? What do we want them to say? What impression do we want to leave with them?"

Because that becomes your reputation, and then over time it becomes your brand. First the reputation is what people think clearly; the brand is the instinctive response. For example, lot of research on this: Sony.

When you think of Sony, what do you think? High-quality electronics. Sony can charge 30-40% for the same product that some other company sells using the same components from the same manufacturer.

You put the Sony name on it, the price is worth 30-40%. This brings us to the final point about branding. The best definition I ever saw: "Branding is composed of two elements. Element number one is the promise you make when you ask the customer to buy from you. Element number two is the promise you keep."

So always remember that it's the promise you make and the promise you keep. It's easy to make promises to get people to buy. You can give them discounts, you can deceive them, you can tell them all kinds of wonderful things to get them to buy, but it's the promise you keep that they remember.

When they say, "Yes, you did keep your promise. Yes, it did work. Yes, the food was delicious. Yes, the product was effective. You delivered on your promises and by gum, I'm going to buy again and tell my friends."

GREG: I love it. So now, Brian, as we close out this section I really want to wrap up the sales, the marketing, and the branding, and I want to give everyone listening some actionable steps, because I really want them to take away- as soon as they hit pause- I want them to turn to their team members and have an action plan they can go after. What can they do right now to really start marketing their business, selling their products, and integrating the brand into that?

BRIAN: Well, you've heard the 80/20 rule. I've said before that marketing and selling is the jelly in the jelly donut. It's the 80% that accounts for everything. Everything else you do in the business is the bread part of the jelly donut.

If you are serious about your business, then you think about marketing which is attracting people who are interested, who have a need, a want, a desire, and selling, which is persuading them to buy from you rather than someone else who can satisfy the same need.

Marketing is attracting qualified prospects; selling is converting them. Every company- 95% of companies- can be better at this. If you're not really good at selling, get good at selling.

Listen to the best audio programs, take the courses, read the books; your ability to convert interested prospects into customers determines your entire life. Here's the wonderful thing: all marketing skills are learnable.

All sales skills are learnable. All business skills are learnable. You can learn every skill you need to learn in order to achieve any business goal you can set for yourself, but you've got to become deadly serious about marketing and attracting new people.

Forget all the little nonsense that you do during the course of the day. There's a beautiful line that says, "Social networking is social not working"; this is not a way of generating customers, it's a way of having communications with people. If you develop a customer after ten years, God bless you.

Your job is to get out there and talk to customers; talk to them on the Internet, talk to them on the phone, talk to them person-to-person, but your job is to be literally obsessed with contacting, communication, and talking to customers, explaining to them why they will be so much better off than they are now if they buy your product or service, and you must do this from dawn to dusk.

Do your paperwork before 8:00 in the morning and after 6:00 at night, and between eight and six do nothing but think about attracting and converting people into buying what you sell.

GREG: That's really, really powerful information that you just shared. Go back, and if you need to learn some selling skills, go learn it. Find the master in sales that you can learn from; find the master in marketing, find the master in business, and really improve those areas in your business.

Go back into Brian's seven areas of the marketing mix and look at all those, and again, look at how you can insert your products and services into that marketing mix and really get the results that you want out of your business.

So go through your Action Guide, and we will see you again in the next section.

Module 3: Building An Everlasting Business

GREG: Hi, this is Greg Rollett and welcome back to the series on building a thriving business in today's economy. Today we've been joined by the legendary Brian Tracy.

Brian's been sharing some of his best secrets to creating a business that is successful in using marketing, media, PR, and branding to really get your business in the position it needs to be in order to be more successful. Here in this section we're going to be talking about recession-proofing your business and building a business that has a lasting legacy.

I really wanted to start by talking about your business, because your business has been able to survive through multiple presidents and different economic situations and different price points for your products. How do you think you've been able to really survive and change and continue to grow through all these different circumstances?

BRIAN: You hear a lot about innovation today; innovation and creativity. Basically, what it means is you're constantly looking for faster, newer, better, easier, cheaper, more convenient ways to generate revenues.

The key to the success of your business is cash flow. If you have positive cash flow, you survive. If you have negative cash flow for any period of time, you die.

As Jack Welch, the CEO of General Electric, once said, if there's anything that you would do to save your business if worse came to worst, don't wait; do it now.

Throw everything off the ship to keep the ship afloat. Lay people off, fire people, cut back, but remember this: there's a great piece of work called *Profit From the Core*, and I teach it all over the place.

Basically what it says it that a business starts off with a core product or service that the business owner and people are good at producing and it's profitable, and that's where every business starts, whether it's cookies or donuts or something else.

Then they begin to expand, and as they expand, they tend to expand into areas that they hope will be really profitable, but often are not as profitable as the core business.

Then they expand into other areas, and this s the natural tendency of companies, to keep expanding into areas that are not as profitable as the core business, and if they're not careful, what they do is they take their eye off the ball and their competitors go in and grab the core business.

So when the market starts to turn down, what you have to do is you have to pull back in like an army camp; pull your soldiers back in to defend the core. You have to start discontinuing all low-profit, no-profit activities and do it quickly.

Get your ego out of the way; we're talking about survival here. Get your ego out of the way and get back to those products and services. As they say, "Dance with the one what brought you."

Get back to the products and services that were the ones you established your business on, and make sure that your business is profitable. Cash flow, positive cash flow, is everything, and you as the business owner are 100% responsible for the survival of your business.

You must make any decisions, any hard decisions, any cold decisions, but you've got to assure survival, and that means you've got to have cash. You've got to pay down debt; you've got to insist on payment from your customers; you've got to negotiate better and tougher terms; you've got to do everything to assure survival.

If you have that mindset, then the next thing you do is say, "What other products or services could we introduce to the market that are an extension, a logical extension, of our key skills, our core competencies, what we do really well?"

Like a McDonald's can bring out a salad or a McRib or something else; they're not starting a donut business across the street, they're doing a natural and logical brand extension or product/service extension from what they're already good at.

As a matter of fact, there's a little book that's called *Small Bets*, and what is says is you don't have to bet your whole company; experiment with one small new product and see how the market response. The rule is: the only test is a market test. The only true test is a customer test.

By the way, a great way we teach this, to test a product or service, is if you have a good idea, call one of your customers and say, "Look, I've got a good idea for this product or service. What do you think?" Customers are amazing; they will tell you like that, exactly if it's a good idea.

Then you say, "How much would you pay for this? I'd probably have to charge this kind of money in order to bring it to the market. How much would you pay?" They'll say, "That's a reasonable price," or "No, I wouldn't pay that much," or "I'd pay even more than that if it will actually do what you say it will do."

You talk to ten customers and they will show you how to recession-proof your business. The other thing is the hardest thing to do is to get a new customer. The easiest thing to do is to take a satisfied customer and sell them more stuff.

The easiest thing beyond that is to get referrals from satisfied customers. A good friend of mine was called by a person whose business was going through a recession and said, "What can I do? No matter how much I advertise, I can't seem to attract more business," which is quite common.

He said, "Go back to every customer you've had for the last two or three years and tell them, 'Thank you for your business; would you like to buy some more?'" The guy went back and did that; within 60 days he increased his sales 40%; went from being in the red to being in the black.

He said he could not believe how much extra business there was just by asking his happy customers to buy some more. Then he said, "Would you happen to know anybody else who might be interested in what we sell?" and he started to get a river of referrals and new business.

He reduced his advertising and promotion, he put all of his focus and time and telephone calls and personal visits on his existing good customers, and they saved his life.

That's one of the most wonderful things you can do, is of course get new businesses with new products and services, but take fabulous care of your existing customers and get them to buy more.

GREG: That's a great, great strategy because there's really this money just sitting there.

BRIAN: Yes, because they already know you. They already like you; they already trust you; they've already given you money; they've already enjoyed your product or service. Say, "Hey, come on down and do it again!"

GREG: Something that I want to talk about, especially in today's economy and today's age, is attention. We sort of talked a little bit about this in marketing, that our attention spans are shorter, we have sites like

YouTube that instead of watching a 30-minute TV show, we're watching a 3-minute video clip.

You have technology that's increasing and just the amount of content that's needed to put out there. Just yourself, you're doing blog posts; you're doing videos; you're doing speaking; you're writing books. There's just a lot that goes into keeping a customer's attention. Can you talk about how that affects business today?

BRIAN: You have to realize that 99% of the time people think about themselves; that a person is more concerned about a split fingernail that they have that they want to get repaired than if 100,000 people are washed out into the ocean in a flood in Bangladesh.

So therefore, if you want to hold people's attention, you have to keep answering the question "What's in it for me?" What's in it for me? What's in it for me? If you want to get people's attention, you have to constantly be addressing what it is that they want and what they need and what they care about.

It's interesting; they will show photographs to men or women to find out what causes pupil dilation, because pupil dilation is the very best indicator of interest. When a person sees something of interest, their pupils dilate.

You know what they find that causes men's pupils to dilate the fastest? Of course, it's pictures of attractive women. What causes women's pupils to dilate is pictures of babies. It's automatic; you show those pictures.

I only tell you that example because your description of your product or service has got to cause pupil dilation. It's got to cause people to pay attention, jerk awake, because it's connecting with something that they really want and need and care about; a pain that they have or a goal they want to achieve.

If you can offer that, then you'll get their attention, and if you keep offering that, like for example we used to say that if you can get people to say 'yes' six times in a sales presentation, then they'll buy your product.

Six 'yes's and they become like a little dog. So I would be selling investments, and I say, "Would you like to see an investment that'll pay you a tremendous rate of return with no risk?" "Absolutely."

"Would you like to become financially independent?" "Yes." "Would you like to have investment that is better than what you have already?" These are the same questions. "Yes."

"Would you like to have an investment that you can afford us to manage for you so it assures high returns?" "Yes." "Would you want an investment that will enable you to sleep well at night because you don't have to worry about it?" "Yes."

It's the same question asked six different times; it's six different benefits of making a good investment. If the person says yes, by the time they've said yes the sixth time, their buying temperature is buying and they want to use your product or service.

Really good advertising and promotion keeps addressing the fundamental need; with regard to money, it's for security and growth. That's what people want. They keep repeating, "Would you like more security? More growth? More growth? More security?" Growth and security; security and growth.

The other person is saying "Yes, yes, yes, yes," and it's the same thing with beautiful foods and lovely restaurants and beautiful decor and lovely lighting and wonderful service and beautiful dishware and fabulous food; it's all a description of the restaurant.

As long as you're describing what the customer wants and needs and is willing to pay for emotionally as well as logically, you'll have their total attention.

GREG: I like that a lot. Attention is very, very important. As we talk about a business that we want to last, there are things that we're going to have to do on a day-to-day basis in order for out business to be here one year, five years, ten years, twenty years down the road.

We've talked about goals, we've talked about marketing, we've talked about sales, but what are some things that business owners really need to think about on a day-to-day basis that are going to impact them years down the road and make sure they're profitable?

BRIAN: Here's an important point: life, as you say, is the study of attention. Therefore, what business owners pay attention to largely determines the direction of their business. It's like the guidance system in the guided missile.

If business owners pay attention to social media, then the company will go nowhere. If business owners are obsessed with selling, obsessed with top line, top line, top line- good business owners are asking every hour: "How much did we sell?"

Every day: "What were our sales today?" Every week: "How much cash do we have in the bank?" Every month: "What were our sales and profitability?"

Whatever the business owner pays attention to the most, that's the direction the whole company goes in. Everybody follows the lead of the business owner, so therefore if you want to build a long-term business, one of the things that we talk about is you've got to get control of your debt.

You've got to have no debt or low debt, and the only debt you have should be debt that is serviceable by your positive cash flow. The businesses that succeed the most are the ones that have cash.

Did you know that Apple is sitting on $50 billion in cash today? That Microsoft is sitting on $46 billion in cash? These are the most successful companies in the world; they have choices.

They can plan for the future; they can invest in new products and services because they have cash in the bank. So you as the business owner: pay attention to the cash.

How much cash? Pay attention to the sales; how much revenue? Pay attention to the receivables. Pay attention to the payables.

It's the most important thing you can do because you build a long-term business by building a really strong short-term business. You build your business day-by-day, week-by-week, month-by-month; it'll build itself year-by-year.

GREG: I love it; I think that's great information to leave you guys on today as we wrap up this third and final section. What I encourage you to do is really go back and listen to everything that Brian has shared with you and really start to apply it to your business.

It's only those that take action that get results, and that's a really, really strong part of this course. Brian's given you some actionable tips, strategies, and things that you can turn around and implement right now in your business, day to day.

Get that cash flow going and you're going to see a very successful business in the future. Brian, I want to thank you for joining us today.

Again, I encourage you guys to take action, and we look forward to seeing your successful businesses for years to come.

Module 4: Separating You From Your Business

GREG: Hi, and welcome to today's program. My name is Greg Rollett and joining me today is Business Credit Expert and the founder of *Credit 360 Consulting* and *Credit 360 Business Funding*, Marco Salinas.

Throughout this program Marco, along with Brian Tracy have put together their years of experience working with businesses all over the world to help you form the success you desire in both your business and life.

Marco is a consumer and business credit expert, and he's a certified *FICO* professional. He's been working in the credit industry for over four years now and has been a speaker on the topic of credit for the last two and a half years.

Here in this first module we're going to be breaking down the necessary actions of actually separating you from your business as we learn about the importance of business credit.

Marco, welcome to the program.

MARCO: Thank you very much.

GREG: Marco, in our talking before we started this program I learned you really truly care about the businesses you're working with. You're able to help them take that next step in their evolution.

I wanted to talk a little of how you first got into this field and why you have a passion for helping businesses succeed in today's market place.

MARCO: Absolutely, Greg.

I really appreciate you giving me this opportunity to discuss with our listeners exactly why I do what I do and how this all came about. It really means a lot to me.

Growing up as a kid I was always one of those types of people who had that entrepreneurial spirit. I knew I wanted to own a business and was always real big on the whole lemonade stand, if you will, type of thing when I was a kid.

After I got out of high school my first semi-official business was an *eBay* business I had, which was more just a trial and error kind of a thing where I was able to learn some things.

I didn't go anywhere with it too much. I did make a little bit of money at that time. I was a young kid enjoying what I was doing and didn't really have any personal big obligations.

Fast forward a few years later. I was now a young father and husband taking care of my family. My priorities in life were obviously a little different now that I had my own people to care for.

My viewpoints on things were also very different.

I found myself going along with the rat race, if you will. I worked regular jobs and kind of got away from my whole entrepreneurial spirit I had.

There was always a voice inside of me as I was doing that. It kept calling me back to getting back into the entrepreneurial world and trying to pursue my dreams of really and truly being a business owner.

During that time frame my wife was going to school full time. She was trying to finish getting her degree to become a teacher. She was working as well.

Her income was not very strong and my job wasn't either. I wanted us to be able to try and get ahead.

Again, I was outside of the idea of the business owner field. Back in the whole of idea of "if you want more money you've got to get out there and work another job." That's how you make extra money.

At the time we also had quite a bit of debt. We wanted to get rid of this debt so we had to make some drastic changes in our life to do that.

It meant moving in with family members so that we could save. I got a second job to try and bring in some extra money. Then I got a third job.

At that point in time I essentially had no life. All I did was work.

I would start my day at about nine in the morning. I would come home after midnight at one in the morning. I would kiss my little kids on the head, kiss my wife, go to bed and then start my day over again.

It was actually quite a torturous time period for me. Again, I still had that little voice that was calling me back, but I had tucked it away and pushed it under.

I said, "There's no way I can do that. I'm a dad and I've got to provide for my family. That's why I'm out here working hard at three job." I was so horribly unhappy with the way things were.

It got to a point where as we were trying to pay off our debt, we were listening to one of the popular financial expert who's on the radio today. One of the things he actually advised was that people should consider working, believe it or not, delivering pizza.

He says, "You can make money that day. You can make up to fifteen to eighteen dollars an hour in tips. You can take that money, apply it towards your debt and get out of debt really quick."

It sounded really appealing to me. Delivering pizzas was by no means anything fun or exciting, or anything you ever would want to bring about, but it was something I was willing to do for my family to try and get out of our debt situation and get back on our feet.

All the while I'm doing this it was really taking a toll on my family life. I was away, gone all the time. I was coming home burned out and exhausted. I really didn't have any days off. I wasn't spending time with my family and it really took its toll.

I remember one night in particular. It was a typical dark and cold November night.

I was out on the streets delivering pizza. I remember going and giving this individual their pizza at this apartment complex.

As I was walking back towards my vehicle, I turned around and all of the sudden I found myself with a gun barrel staring me in my face. I was obviously being robbed at gunpoint.

I remember I stood still there for a moment as I was staring at this individual holding this gun at me. A lot of things were going through my mind during this critical moment.

I'm thinking to myself "Is this guy going to pull the trigger? Is this it? Is this how I'm going to leave this place doing something like delivering pizza? Is this the way I would want to be remembered?"

I remember thinking to myself, "There's got to be a better place. There's got to be a better way. I can't do this any longer."

This person ended up robbing me for fifteen dollars. That's all I had in cash including the tip in my pocket. This person was willing, obviously, to do that for such a small amount of money.

It made me realize I needed to make some changes in my life. That wasn't even the worst part. The worst part of this whole situation was that I was in such a bad financial place at that time that I didn't even call the police like most people would have done.

I felt like I had no choice but to get in my car and drive back to the store. I went in there and told the manager what had happened. The worst part of all was I had to turn back around, go right back out there and keep doing what I was doing.

I felt I didn't have a choice to leave that job. I felt like I needed every penny I could get at that moment in time because I was so desperate to pay off my debt.

I was so desperate to get out of that living situation we were in while living with family because it was so challenging and difficult for me, and my family.

I felt trapped. It was the worst feeling in the world.

I went back out there. I was paranoid and afraid. I thought I was going to get robbed again on that same night.

I just kept thinking to myself as that night went on, "I can't do this. This is horrible. This is a horrible thing."

"What happened to you, Marco? What happened to the drive you had? What happened to those feelings you had where you were going to be a business owner and do great things?"

"Look where you've ended up. You've ended up in this place where you work all day long. You don't really make a whole lot of money and now you're even having to risk your life for this little extra change you're bringing home."

I came home that night. Again, I kissed my family.

I couldn't tell my wife. That was the worst part. I couldn't tell her because I knew she was going to say, "You need to get out of there. You can't do that."

Inside I really felt I couldn't quit that job. I had to keep that from her until after I ended up quitting that job later down the road a few months later.

That was a horrible place. And as I lay down on the pillow that night I told myself, "I will make a change. I will get myself to a different place."

"When I get to that place, one of my goals and objectives is to help others so that they don't have to end up in a situation where their only option is to work three jobs."

"And if they have that entrepreneurial spirit and drive, and they want to start their own business, but there are road blocks, what can I do to help them overcome those road blocks so they can follow their dreams and take that step into being a business owner?"

It is a scary step, a scary jump and a scary leap.

But, do you know what? It's a lot less scary than being out there on the streets having guns pointed at your face when you're just trying to make some extra money for your family.

GREG: Marco, that's a very, very powerful story.

I think a lot of small business owners can relate to some of the situations you've been faced with. I can really see now why you have a passion for helping people get out of these situations and to ultimately have the lifestyle and business they truly deserve.

Throughout this program we're going to be talking about how they can take that next level and combine them with Brian Tracy's building strategies. We're going to help them get to a place of success in their lives.

Here in this first module we're going to be talking the separation of your personal finances and the finances of your company or business.

This is really a very vital first step, especially when you have that young family, when you have a savings account and things like that.

Let's start at the beginning. What do most business owners currently think and believe about what business credit really is?

MARCO: Before I get into that, Greg, I do just want to make a quick note of how emotional I am right now. This is such an amazing…well, the best word to use is blessing.

It's just an absolute blessing to be able to have the opportunity to partner up with literally a living legend, which is Brian Tracy.

Knowing that I've been in the trenches and some really difficult places in my life, and being able to now partner up with a such an amazing individual and offer this product to others who want to really take their business to the next level or who just want to get their business started, it's just a very, very overwhelming opportunity.

I'm so grateful for that opportunity.

We are very much dedicated to helping those we come in contact with to really excel in what they do. Again, as you talked about, one of those big factors is the separation of the personal finances from the finances of the company.

Most business owners right now usually believe one of two things. Either they believe building business credit is something that easily happens automatically, or they feel like no matter what kind of debt of expenses they incur for their business all has to always be attached to their personal finances and credit report.

The best part of this whole system is that this is not true. You can truly separate you and your personal credit from your business and any debts that your business is incurring.

That is absolutely the first step of this process. It's to learn how to go about doing that and making sure you're protecting you and your family from the possibility of having all this business debt on your side.

There's no reason why you shouldn't go and take the steps to separate those two because most businesses don't do that. Most business owners unfortunately end up with a lot of personal liabilities attached to their own personal credit report.

It doesn't have to be that way, Greg.

GREG: What I want to do now is help everyone listening to paint a picture of what this separation looks like and what it can mean to a small business.

I know you have a great story about a business that had an opportunity to grow. They really had success in the palm of their hands but they were held back to a problem many small businesses have, which is cash flow.

They couldn't afford to go out and buy that new equipment that was going to take them to the next level and get them the new orders and business.

I feel like it's a common objective many businesses are feeling. They're thinking, "I have this one new opportunity but I can't get there."

Can you share that story with us and relate it to everybody who's listening?

MARCO: Yes, absolutely.

The fact of the matter is this story is something I hear time and time again. It's not so much just one individual story. I hear this story repeated all the time.

The story ultimately goes that an individual has worked hard. They've built their business, they've got business coming in and things are going well.

Many times they end up in a place where they are starting to get noticed by others who are interested in their service. Sometimes those that are interested in their service are people who might be requesting a little more than what that small business can handle.

I've seen, for instance, an individual that had a tow truck business and owned a couple of tow trucks. First of all, all of those tow trucks were on his personal credit. We're talking about some pretty heavy duty debt that's attached to his personal credit report and is completely lop siding his debt to income ratios.

If he wanted to purchase a home, he would have a really difficult time doing so because all of those tow trucks were attached to his credit report.

The problem is also that he's going to get maxed out pretty quickly if he needs to get another truck of piece of equipment for that truck because he completely thinned out his resources on his personal credit.

If he had business credit, that debt should have been over on that side, on the business side of it.

As it's on the business side it's going to open up the door to a lot more opportunities as far as the actual funding.

So, if he's got two trucks and he needs a third one, if he was to compare trying to get a third one, his personal credit compared to trying to get it on the business credit, it's going to be a lot smoother of a process if he's trying to get it on the business side.

Again, that's just one example. I've seen individuals who own landscaping companies and want to buy the latest greatest lawn equipment so they could get more work done and more jobs.

They could possibly get bigger commercial accounts and things like that. With some of their smaller equipment there's no way in the world they'd be able to do that.

Being able to get access to that extra capital is going to allow them, like you said, to really take things to the next level. Whereas normally if they didn't have this opportunity to build business credit, the answer would probably be "no."

"Hey, I'd like to hire you to do this? Can you do it?"

"No, I can't. I don't have that capital. I don't have that equipment and I'm stuck. I have to stay where I'm at right now, wait another couple of years to hopefully grow this business slowly to get there."

If they had the business credit they'd be able to obtain that funding and financing to get that equipment, accept that job and probably pretty quickly pay off any debt that was incurred to purchase that equipment because of that job they took.

GREG: Marco, I want to thank you for sharing that story because I think a lot of business owners listening right now are going through a situation very, very similar.

What I want to do now is talk about some of the key differences between business and personal debt.

I want everyone listening to do as Marco is going through these differences, have out a sheet of paper, have out your action guide, and go ahead and start writing down some of these differences.

You'll really start to see it and how it relates to your business.

Marco, what are some of the differences between your personal credit, personal debt, and business debt?

MARCO: The big difference is, first of all, business credit is credit that's obtained in the business name.

Again, traditionally and I know with myself personally, I started my business and got a letter in the mail just like most people do when they get a business credit card advertisement.

It said it was a *Capital One Business Credit Card*. At that time I was actually very blurry on the topic of business credit. It was frustrating to me because I knew everything there was to know about consumer credit but business credit was something I had a lot of opportunity to learn about.

We started getting more and more of our customers on the consumer credit side that said, "Marco, teach me more about business credit. I want to learn more. I want to learn how to build business credit."

Basically myself and my business partner, Jay, had to go out and get as much information as we could and cram ourselves with as much about business credit and how the system works, which is basically what we're sharing with you here today.

Again, the main difference is that business credit is obtained in the actual business name compared to that credit card I was just mentioning.

I applied for it. I got approved. I got my little *Capital One Business Card.* It said the name of my business on the credit card, but about a month later I looked at my credit report and of course that credit card was on my credit report.

I remember thinking to myself, "OK, so this is a business credit card. Why is it on my credit account, my personal credit report?"

That's where I really started realizing and learning most people's business credit is still attached to their personal side. So, true business credit is obtained not in Marco Salina's name, but in the name of his business. That's really what happens with business credit.

With business credit the business itself builds its own credit profile and credit score, not the individual. With an established credit profile and an established business credit profile and score, the business will then qualify for greater amounts of business credit.

This credit in the business name is based on the business's ability to pay, not the business owner's. That's the beautiful part.

For most individuals, the business is already established, it's already making some money, it's already got some accounts receivable, and it's already doing things like that.

A lot of times business lenders are able to look at the other criteria for the business itself, not the individual's consumer credit reports, and lend based on those criteria.

Since the business qualifies for the credit, in some cases there's actual no personal credit check required from the business owner.

GREG: Marco, that's a very, very powerful distinction you just took everyone through.

What I want to do now is take everyone and create that shift in their minds because a lot of small business owners aren't yet thinking with some of the knowledge and experience you have in how you just broke that down about this topic of business credit.

Let's go through the first step someone needs to take in order to make that separation to split themselves from their business.

MARCO: Yes, absolutely.

The very first foundational step in this process is going to be incorporating your business.

A lot of the individuals we come in contact with are sole proprietors. As a sole proprietor you can absolutely and one hundred percent build business credit for your business.

The big difference, the big factor there is that whatever funding you receive through your business credit as a sole proprietor, that debt will still be attached to your personal credit report.

Let me say that again. If you are a sole proprietor and you build business credit, you will get it and you will get funding. However, whatever you incur as far as debt for that business will still be personally guaranteed, one hundred percent of it.

The only way to truly separate you from the business is to from a corporation or an *LLC*. This is an incredibly vital step. Not only is it going to help you separate the actual debt from your personal side of the business, but it also has other perks like protection lawsuits and things like that.

If you were to get sued the person suing you cannot come after your personal assets. It really is a vital step.

I've met people that think when you go out and incorporate that it automatically separates the two, your personal credit and business credit. That's not true.

Opening up that corporation is the first step but there are several steps beyond that, which we'll be touching on here in the next module. But, doing that and taking that step is vital. It's absolutely vital.

GREG: For someone who is a sole proprietor, whom should they consult with in order to begin forming one of these partnerships or corporations to take that first step?

MARCO: That's a great question.

What we'd like to do is direct everyone over to a resources webpage called *BusinessCreditTools.com*. This is the resources page, which is going to have a list of the items that are going to assist you in building your business credit.

That first item is, again, opening up that corporation.

You can find a link on there for doing that and you'll be able to take a look at some of the options. Read through there.

I also really recommend you go to your library or the bookstore. One of the things I really enjoying doing is going to the library or going to *Barnes and Noble.*

I'll go into the business section and just glance through some of the books there that talk about starting a small business in your field. Obviously the most important thing is establishing a corporation and deciding what you want to do.

Do you want an *LLC*? Do you want an *S* corporation? Which of these is going to be the best fit for you?

Educate yourself on that topic first. Make sure you're making the right choice.

Visit the website *BusinessCreditTools.com.* You'll be able to go directly there and get that process started.

GREG: Marco, I want to thank you for providing that resource. We'll be touching back on that website as we go throughout this program.

Now we're taking action. We have this new company and this new partnership. We've correctly structured the company we currently have.

Let's talk about how structuring the company properly really gives the company a credit history.

MARCO: Yes.

Here's the important thing to mention. When you go and form that corporation or *LLC*, it's kind of similar to when you graduate from high school or your turn eighteen and start receiving some of these credit card offers in the mail.

The only difference is it's not going to be so much there laid out on a platter as it is for you on the consumer credit side.

The point I'm trying to get at is that as a new corporation, you are starting off with a blank slate. This is a brand new clean slate. It's not going to have any credit built or started on it.

You're starting with nothing and you're going to have to build credit on that new corporation properly.

Again, that's what we'll be outlining here in these steps, especially in the next module we're just about to get into. This is going to show you step-by-step the foundational steps beyond the corporation or the *LLC* that are needed to get this process going so you can really separate yourself from the business and the business debt.

GREG: Marco, we're making this decision. We're starting to build the credit history of the company.

I know we've touched on it, but I really want to wrap our heads around what the actual opportunity is for businesses now that they're making this mindset adjustment, they're separating themselves from the business, they're going and setting up these companies.

Marco, what is the big picture? What's the big opportunity that we now present ourselves with by going through these steps?

MARCO: Well, the big opportunity here is now this business credit is being built and you are going to have the opportunity to have access to the funding you need.

One of the key things we talk about is once you establish business credit and once you obtain funding, it doesn't always necessarily mean you have to take every single bit of what you've been offered.

It's always good to know you have access to it. It's like the example we talked about a little while ago where maybe you own a landscaping company and you've got a big commercial account that says, "I want you guys to work on this."

It's going to be a big opportunity for that small business owner. If they have to turn that down because they can't get access to a couple of mowers or a larger piece of equipment, ultimately they're going to have to say "no," and turn that down.

With this opportunity here essentially what we're doing is giving the business owner double the borrowing power as they have both their personal and business credit profiles built.

This is a real game changer for a lot of people to have this and knowledge. It's a peace of mind that knowing the business credit being built is not attached to their personal file.

That should really bring a lot of peace to many business owners knowing that those two items are completely separate.

GREG: Marco, I really want to thank you for sharing that big opportunity that everyone listening can think about the big picture of what is possible for their business.

As we wrap up here in this first module, Marco, what is the one thing every business owner needs to do now right when this recording ends?

I want people to take action. They're only going to get the success and results from their life and businesses if they actually take action on this content.

What can they do now to truly separate themselves financially from their business?

MARCO: Again, I want to reiterate what I mentioned just a little while ago.

You really need to take the time to research and make sure you're making the right decision as far as the business entity you would like to start, whether it is the corporation or the *LLC*.

Again, spending time at the library looking up these books and doing some research online, figuring out in your state and the type of business you have which of these situations is going to be best for you as far as taxes and obviously income opportunities, and what's going to help you be the most profitable.

Make sure you really are making the best decision possible on that. From there, visit that resources page we talked about, which is going to be in the action guide as well. It's *BusinessCreditTools.com*.

You will be able to go in there and also find out about what corporation or *LLC* may be best for you and how to go about starting and forming that to get that process going.

If you've already got that done then you want to definitely make sure you follow along with the next module and have everything in place correctly.

GREG: I really do think that's a great place for everyone listing now to begin.

What I encourage you to do is go back through your action guide for module one. Go through all the different exercises, tips and resources that Marco has laid out for you.

Once you complete that I want you to join us again in module two where Marco's going to break down your business credibility building process, as well as how to build credit for your business to help you get to the places you want to take your business.

Thanks again for listening to module one. Go through your action guide, take some action and we will see you again in module two.

Module 5: Business Credibility Building Process

GREG: Welcome back to the second module on building your business and finding the financial assistance you need in order to have your business break through and serve more people.

Here in this second module we're going to be talking about how you as a business owner can raise your credit profile of the business.

As we begin, Marco, let's talk about what business credibility is and why it's so important for those looking to get funding for their business.

MARCO: Business credibility is an absolutely essential step in obtaining business credit and business funding and financing.

A potential creditor, a potential lender or a potential vendor will look at your business' ability to build strong business as their criteria for deciding if they want to lend you money or not.

The perception they receive from your business plays a huge role in that process.

We've all heard the phrase "perception is reality." That really does hold true with the business credit building process.

Thanks to the technology available to us today there are a lot of amazing available resources out there to help a small business look and feel a lot larger than what it really is.

It can actually give them some of those competitive components if you will that some of their larger counter parts have, such as the 1-800 numbers of the fancy phone prompts when you call into the business and things like that.

Those things are available now and are much easier for the small business whereas maybe ten years ago it pretty much didn't even exist. This is truly to the benefit of the small business owner now, especially in this business credit building process.

That's what we're going to be talking about. We're going to outline those business credibility-building steps that are essentially vital to having in place.

Again, before applying for business credit the business needs to ensure it at least meets if not exceeds all of the lender credibility standards. There are quite a few of them.

We're going to touch of those key component ones. They break down to about thirteen of them. That's what we're going to go ahead and be touching here in this module.

GREG: What we're going to do now is put a little bit of the focus on to the lender and the thirteen key points or factors we're going to be looking at in just a minute.

Why is it so important from the lender side that they look at these different points?

MARCO: Again, this is the perception that the lender has of your business. This is the way it looks on that side looking over towards you.

It needs to look very credible. It needs to look legitimate. It needs to look like something that is stable and strong.

If these potential lenders are going to give anyone funding, obviously they want to make sure they're giving it to an organization, company or business where they're going to get their return and their money back with their interest.

Obviously there's always a risk for them. If the business looks shaky or it's missing some of these key components, these are going to be big red flags.

They're basically going to jump ship right away and say, "No way, no how am I going to lend this guy money if he doesn't even have these basic component steps in place."

It is vitally important to have these things in place.

If you ask, "Where did these come from?" This information is really through trial and error. It's from others that have gone before you and have tried to obtain this, have done it the wrong way and then learned from their mistakes.

That's essentially what we're doing. We're putting this information together. This is tried and true and tested stuff.

We know it works and that's essentially where it comes from.

GREG: Alright Marco, so we talked about why lenders are looking at these different points and even where some of them come from.

For the small business owner they're like, "Marco, another thirteen steps or thirteen things I need to do in my business…" Do we really need to have all of them in place before looking to get business credit?

MARCO: The short answer to that, Greg, is absolutely.

Some of these things seem like they're not even going to make a whole lot of sense. They seem a little unimportant, if you will. But, I can't emphasize to you enough how vital each and every one of these steps is.

The key word is foundation. If you build a home and the foundation of the home is not built properly, what good does it do to have the first, second or third floor with all the greatest and latest construction equipment on the planet if the foundation is built wrong? It's still going to crumble.

The same is true for the business credit process. You need to make sure you cross every one of these items off the list. Obviously some of them are going to be a little more important than others.

But, in my opinion and what I've seen, every one of these are definitely still worth the time to make sure you take care of and cross each and every one of them off the list.

GREG: Let's jump right in and help all the small business owners start to check these off the list. I really want to prepare them to be able to get this credit as soon as possible.

We started to go over some of these in module one, but the first two factors are business name and corporate identity. So, what are we specifically looking for here in order to boost our business credibility?

MARCO: Having the exact legal business name including the recorded *DBA* filing is vitally important to the business credit process.

Some business owners have their businesses set up as "*X-Y-Z LLC*" as the name of the actual company. Others have the business set up as "*X-Y-Z Corporation* doing business as *X-Y-Z Muffler shop*."

There are some variances there. If you set your business up one way with the *DBA*, essentially what you need to do is have that set up that way all over the place. The records need to be filed exactly the same no matter where you're at, no matter what you're doing.

If your one account shows it as "*X-Y-Z Corporation* doing business as *X-Y-Z Muffler Shop*," and then you've got another one that just says "X-Y-Z Muffler Shop," what you're doing is creating multiple credit files.

If you have multiple credit files open all you're going to do is create total chaos. And it's just going to create more frustration for you.

This information needs to be cleaned up and reported exactly the way the legal business name is, including again the *DBA* filing if you have one.

It may not seem like a gigantic step but it is extremely important because again, you don't want to open up multiple credit files. That's going to create a lot of headaches, a lot of chaos and a lot of issues.

GREG: Next on the list is the EIN number. That seems pretty standard and most businesses should be pretty good to go there.

Moving on to number four is a business address.

So, Marco, what are we looking for here? What happens if we're running our business from home, or a shared location or space? Maybe we've just moved in and we don't have a longstanding lease agreement or lease terms.

How do all of these factors relate to our business credibility?

MARCO: The business address is going to be one of the most important steps of the process.

A lot of small business owners do start their business from the ground up, and in doing so end up beginning to start the business as an at-home type of a business. That's Ok because there's nothing wrong with that.

But, in the eyes of the lender the business needs to have a real address.

Now, what's a real address? Let's start off with what a real address is not.

A real address is not a home address, obviously. A real business address is not a PO Box. Not even a *UPS* store address is going to qualify you either.

It needs to be a real brick and mortar building with a deliverable, physical address. In our day in age there are so many options are far as opening up a business address, especially now with the movement of the virtual office.

The virtual office works as far as building the business credit. So, take advantage of that. There are some of these resources you can tap into where you can open up a virtual office, you'll have the professional address, you'll have the mailbox where you can receive mail and it still counts.

You can use that as your business address even though you may never go to that office. You're only using it as a mailbox.

It's still going to be worth it and it's still a vital, vital step. So, you can do the address only. You can do the virtual office where you can actually go there from time to time.

Obviously the most important and the biggest one is if you have a true office. But, all three of those criteria work in the business credibility building process.

GREG: Marco, the next few ones I want to spend a few minutes on is that we should be listed in 4-1-1. You should also have a toll free 1-800 number, as well as a dedicated fax line.

Can you talk about these, their importance and how to get them if we don't have them yet in place?

MARCO: Absolutely.

4-1-1 is one of those criteria I like to talk about a lot because, again, people think 4-1-1 is kind of an unimportant steps in this process particular, and especially with the younger generation.

When you talk to a young business owner some of them won't even really know what 4-1-1 is. Obviously they know all about *Google* and about all the great resources available online, but 4-1-1 is something that is still used in the business credit building process.

You can't write it off. And as of today it's still a very important step.

You must have a dedicated business number listed with 4-1-1 directory assistance under the business name. Lenders, vendors, creditors, and even insurance providers will verify that your business is actually listed with 4-1-1.

There mentality is if you're not even at least listed there, your business is pretty much not even real. You're just some little home operator that doesn't really care about showing you are credible.

I can't stress to you enough. Some of these revolving accounts such as *Staples* for example, can do applications over the phone but they're still going to gather your info. They're going to put you on hold, pick up the phone and call 4-1-1.

If you're not listed in the directory they're going to pick the phone back up and tell you, "I am sorry. Your application has been denied," for that one reason alone.

You can see just how vital this step is.

Transitioning from the 4-1-1, you do want to have a toll free number that you can add to that 4-1-1 directory listing. You also need to have a local business number as well that you can add to that 4-1-1 directory listing.

Do not use your home phone or your cell phone. That is not the place to put your number into that system. You need to get established with these resources.

Nowadays it is incredibly affordable. You can find links and resources to establishing these types of services through our resources page I talked about earlier, *BusinessCreditTools.com.*

Moving on, the next on I want to emphasize again is phone and fax. Fax is another one of those topics I here people say, "Fax machine? That's a '90's tool. People don't use fax machines any more."

Well, in the business credit process a fax machine is still an incredibly important component. A lot of these business credit companies will offer the application, approvals and things like that through the fax. They want to receive the information as well through the fax.

One of the things they're going to check is if you have a fax line in place. You must have that information in place. It is vitally important.

So, after you establish your 1-800 number, the next thing you want to do is also establish an actual dedicated fax line. Nowadays with these fax numbers you don't need to have on old-fashioned gigantic fax machine sitting on the table because these systems are now all done through the *Cloud.*

They are actually affordable. There is a very low monthly fee to keep the system going. I can't emphasize to you enough to keep that in place because, again, lenders and creditors on the business credit side view see this as a key component in the business credit building process.

You will need that fax number to receive those important documents like the credit applications. It's something you cannot overlook.

GREG: That was a really good distinction on those three areas.

The next two we're going to talk about are a website and an email address. I think the majority of everyone going through this program know what a website and an email address is.

But, what's really going to help us in the eyes of the credit lenders?

MARCO: This seems like such a common thing nowadays, the whole website and email thing.

Greg, you'd be amazed how many people either don't have a professional website or a professional email setup, or they have something in place but it's actually quite sloppy.

If you have a basic little website and all it has is one page with a couple of lines with your phone number and address, that's probably nowadays not going to cut it.

You need to have a fully set up website with at least a few pages. I like to tell people to have at least five pages setup with a little bit of information. It doesn't have to be elaborate or over the top.

It just needs to be several pages with some key components about what you're company does, what separates you from your competition, and then of course a page with your address and phone number. You can put your 1-800 number and your fax number.

If all that stuff is on there and the potential lender looked up your information and they got to your website and found it again, all it's going to do is just reiterate the credibility you have established.

The website doesn't need to be up and running for a long time for this to work. You can set it up and have it in place, if they check it a week later so what? It's good to go. You're ready.

The key thing to focus on is you need to have it.

The other aspect is people sometimes will start a business and they'll keep using their *Gmail* or *Yahoo* account. *Wildchic22@yahoo.com* is not going to cut it when it comes to trying to build business credibility.

You need to have an email that say *"@yourcomapany.com."* or *"@XYZCorporation.com."* You need to have your email setup as *"support@yourcompanyname.com"* *"info@yourcompany.com,"* or your name – *"John.Doe@yourcompanyname.com"*

This information needs to be setup. And again, free services like *Yahoo*, *Hotmail* or *Gmail* need to go. That is going to create a very bad impression on a potential lender if that's all you have in place.

It's too easy and too inexpensive to neglect this.

GREG: Number eight on our list is licensing. What does this mean and what's going to help us out here?

MARCO: One of the most common mistakes when building credit for your company is not matching business address on your business license.

That is one of the things people do. They get the licensing that's required for their business, whatever kind of business they're in, but the business address is not on there. Instead they have their home address listed or a PO Box listed.

You do want to make sure you have the business address on those licensing. Potential business credit lenders may go and pull that information. They want to see that business address on there and they want to see it matching up. That is a big step for them.

Even worse, though, is not having the required licenses for your type of business to operate legally.

Some people become very complacent. They start making money and begin overlooking those key steps to not so much building credit, but just operating their business in compliance.

A lot of businesses out there do require some sort of licensing through the their city or state, or some sort of local governing council where you need to have that license in place.

If you don't have that and they go and check, not only are you going to get rejected for business credit, but your business could actually get shut down.

Again, make sure those things are in place. Make sure you have that. That way if anybody checks to make sure you do have a required license or permits in place everything is good to go and you're not hitting any roadblocks on that one topic.

GREG: Number nine is fairly standard and most businesses will have already established this. It's going to be a bank account. It's not just about having a bank account.

How can we help ourselves out with our banking to secure large business loans for our business?

MARCO? The bank account is probably going to be the most important step of this process.

The reason for that is because it's pretty simple. The date you opened your business bank account is pretty much the day the lender considers your business to have started.

The example I like to tell people is back when I had my little *eBay* business it was a small thing. It was a hobby that made a little bit of extra money for me. But, some people were really able to blow their *eBay* business into a huge moneymaking empire.

A lot of those businesses were started through *PayPal*. *PayPal* is a very easy service to get started with when accepting payment.

You have other competitors to *PayPal* nowadays, which are even better like *WePay.com*. It makes that process even easier and smoother.

The only downside to that is people end up taking money and payments through those types of online systems and then that money gets deposited right into their personal bank account.

Sometimes businesses are actually started through this process. They operate sometimes for months or even years. Then finally that person will go out and say, "Do you know what? I'm going to go out and start an official business bank account."

You might have your little *eBay* or online business open for two years, but in the eyes of the lender if you just opened up your business bank account yesterday, your business has been opened for pretty much one day.

You can see how important that is. Your business banking history is vital to your future success of being able to secure larger business loans. That's something you cannot overlook.

GREG: It's very, very important. I appreciate you breaking that down.

As we move on, number ten on our list is business listings. What do you mean here and how can we ensure we are listed constantly and accurately across multiple agencies and directories?

MARCO: This goes back a little bit to what I was talking about as far as making sure you have your legal business name listed correctly with your bank account and tax return.

If you go and get the business lease or office lease that also needs to be matched up correctly.

It's similar to that. You must confirm that every agency, creditors, suppliers, trade credit vendors, and everybody have your business listed the exact same way.

There are some little minor things that can actually kind of throw things off. You want to try and stay on top of it.

Your business name, your address, and your phone should be listed with the exact same spelling. For example, you might have *"X-Y-Z Incorporated"* and another place might have your listed as *"X-Y Consultants,"* or *"X-Y consultants Incorporated."*

All of those three things are going to cause chaos and confusion to the business credit building process. You want to make sure all of that stuff is lined up properly and correctly.

Even simple differences like Suite 500 or just putting #500, or Lot 500 are important. They should be corrected where possible.

Take the time to verify that those main agencies like the state, the *IRS*, the bank, 4-1-1, and those kinds of places have your business listed the same way with your exact legal name.

GREG: That's really, really important, especially to maintain consistency.

I want to talk about every business owner's favorite subject, which is taxes, and more specifically tax returns.

In this step, are we just looking to make sure we have filed here or does it go a little deeper than that?

MARCO: Tax returns are obviously something every business owner is going to have to spend some time on. It's a key component. We all know we have to pay our taxes to the *IRS*.

As far as the actual credit building process and how the taxes are tied in with that, the main thing is you really need to have all your business tax returns filed.

You need to make sure that information is done, it's on record, and that it's filed and listed correctly. If you skip over that, it definitely can open up the door to some potential issues.

That's really the key component. There's not a whole lot to spend time on there. Just make sure you are filing because if you're skipping over some years and not getting that done and turned it, it can potentially cause some issues.

GREG: One thing lenders will want to look into when they're determining the credibility of business are any liens or judgments on a property.

How do we look back into our own public records and make sure we're in the clear?

MARCO: To build business credit you cannot have any outstanding liens are judgments pending against the actual business. If you have that it's going to cause a problem. That information does need to be check.

Most people are going to know, obviously, if they've been sued or have a judgment against them. Or, if you're not paying your taxes and you have a tax lien you're going to pretty well know about it.

You probably want to make sure to take the time to go down to the courthouse or your county's record website to pull that information. Find out the details.

Try your best to get on a payment plan with those guys. Even better, eliminate those debts as quickly as you can. Get that out of the way.

Once those debts are satisfied you pretty well should be smooth sailing, especially if get yourself a release of judgment or release of lien showing that information is taken care of.

That's something you can't overlook. You've got to get that out of the way if you want to build business credit properly.

GREG: It's a very important step.

Here we are at the thirteenth and final factor that could really help or hurt your business credibility. That's your business model.

How much does your business model play a role in your business credibility?

MARCO: This is actually, believe it or not, probably one of the lesser looked at steps, but you still don't want to ignore it.

You want to have at least a simple summary of your business plan with revenue projections in place. It's something that summarizes where you want to go with your business, what your plans are and what you've done so far.

That way if a potential lender does request that, you've got something in place that's ready to go. You can fire that off.

You're going to look more prepared and more credible. Again, that's what this whole entire module is all about.

GREG: That's awesome. I really like bringing that together.

We've covered a lot with these thirteen principle factors. As we wrap up here in this second module, Marco, are there any other things we should be looking out for in order to maintain our good business credibility?

MARCO: Yeah. One of the things I do like to emphasize is that after you go through the steps you're probably going to be signing up for possibly some things you don't have yet such as a new fax line, a new 1-800 number.

A lot of those services are going to require a monthly payment. Even the website will most likely have a monthly fee involved.

You want to make sure you don't neglect those little monthly payments. Some of those things like the website hosting we like and use, if you buy a couple of years in advance, it comes out to basically five dollars a month.

It's not an expensive cost, but it is still a vital cost to you. You want to keep up with these things.

If you pay for web hosting, you let it run out and your lender goes to your website and finds your domain or website it dead, it's only going to cause more slowdowns and more problems with the whole process.

Don't ignore those little monthly fees. Keep your phone line in place and the 1-800 number even though it's maybe only ten dollars a month. It's still a very vital item as we covered.

You want to make sure all that is in place and up and running. And if you're the kind of person that is so busy that you can't do it, take the time to make sure one of your employees does it. You can also hire a virtual assistant to help you with that kind of stuff to stay on top of those things.

Sometimes the little details like that can really cause these deals to go sour. So, don't forget about that kind of basic stuff.

GREG: Marco, we've really covered a lot here in this second module.

What I want to do before we close out here is I was hoping you could just go through those thirteen point again just so we can really create that mental checklist of the things we need to do in our business.

MARCO: Sure.

Let's just recap. Number one was the business name, having the exact legal business name in place including if you do have *DBA* on record.

Number two was corporate entities. Again, separating your business entity from your personal side, the corporation or the *LLC*.

Number three was getting that *EIN* number, making sure you have an *EIN* number in place and making sure you have your business listed with the same tax ID number all over the place.

Number four was the business address, having a real brick and mortar building address in place and not a PO Box or home address.

Number five was really three-in-one, having the 4-1-1, having the 1-800 toll free number and having the dedicated fax line. All three of those are small inexpensive steps but are extremely important to the business credit building process.

Number six was having a website in place that is actually setup and established with a few pages ready to go.

Number seven was having an email in the company name, not *Hotmail*, *Yahoo* or *Gmail*, but a real one like *"@yourcompany.com."*

Number eight would be licensing, making sure you have your proper license in place so you can operate your business legally. And, of course, make sure the information is listed correctly, especially the business address.

Number nine is the bank account. Have that bank account open as soon as possible because, again, the day you open your business bank account is the day your business started in the eyes of the lender.

Number ten would be your business listings. Going back to what we talked about earlier, make sure you have your business listed the same way with all of your places you have it listed and with your exact legal name.

Number eleven is making sure you tax returns are filed and in place.

Number twelve is making sure your public records are listed and cleared, and that you don't have any outstanding liens or judgments against the business.

And number thirteen, the final step, is at least making sure you have a simple summary of your business plan with revenue projects in place.

Those are those key thirteen but very vital and important business credibility-building steps.

GREG: As we wrap up this second module, what I encourage everyone to do is to go back through each of these thirteen factors Marco broke down for you and ensure you have them setup in your business.

If you haven't, create a checklist and just start going through them one by one by one until you've covered all thirteen areas.

Once you've done that I want you to come back and join us in module three where Marco is going to break down the business credit system.

Thanks again for listening to module two. Get to work, take some action and we will see you again in module three.

Module 6: The Business Credit System

GREG: Hi, and welcome back to this third critical module on business credit and funding to help your business take the next step towards becoming a success.

Here in this third module we're going to be talking about the system that delivers the credit as well as the ways to continue to build your assets and business credit score.

Marco, let's begin this third module by talking about the bureaus. Who are they, what is their background and how do they report their business credit scores?

MARCO: That's a very good question and something we need to spend a little bit of time on.

I want to go over exactly whom the bureaus are and exactly what you can do to go about the steps to obtaining your business credit reports and tracking that information so you can see where your business credit is.

There is confusion on the consumer credit side as far as who the three credit bureaus are. On the consumer credit side you have *Experian*, you have *Equifax* and you have *TransUnion*.

On the business credit side, two are involved, but there's a third one that's not. *TransUnion* is not part of the business credit reporting system.

Instead another company called *Dun and Bradstreet* is in there. So, you have *Experian, Dun and Bradstreet* and *Equifax*.

Most small business owners know who *Dun and Bradstreet* is. They are the largest business credit reporting system out there. They also have very aggressive sales teams that target the small business owners and sell their products.

That's a big part of the reason why they're pretty well known.

The most important step in the process is that you want to make sure you get a copy of your business credit report to see what is being reported. If you already have a business in place, you may already have a little bit of business credit built or you may not. That's why it's important to make sure you're getting in there and checking.

The first thing I want to start with is *Experian*. We're also going to list these links in the action guide as well as on our resources web page, *BusinessCreditTools.com*. I am going to talk a little bit about where you need to go to obtain this information.

Experian's website is *SmartBusinessReports.com*. That is where you can get a copy of your smart business report offered through *Experian*.

The cost with *Experian* is usually somewhere between forty-nine to ninety-nine dollars for the Smart Business Report. It's going to allow you to find out how many trade lines you have reporting, see if you have business credit scores already set up, and see if you have an active *Experian* business profile in place. They'll also check to see if you have any recent inquiries.

The cost you pay for that *Experian* business credit report does include an *Experian* credit score. That is the *Experian* process.

You can now purchase a copy of your *Equifax* small business credit report online. There is a good chance your credit profile will not be available through that system.

It typically takes more time to create a file with *Equifax* small business. That's why it's important to apply with the credit providers who report to *Equifax* as well.

The website is a little funny on this one, but it's *Equifax.com/small-business/credit-report/ensb.* Don't worry about trying to write down this information. It's going to be in the action guide and you'll be able to have access to that link in there.

That's $99.95 for the full credit report through *Equifax*.

Let's talk a little about the big guy, *Dun and Bradstreet* and the DUN's number. Obtaining a *Dun and Bradstreet* number, which would be a DUN number begins the process of building your business credit profile with them.

Your actual DUN's number does play a very important role in enabling your business to borrow without a personal guarantor. That's going to be something you definitely want to spend some time on making sure you have your DUN's number set up.

The website to get that is going to be *www.DNB.com.* Because *Dun and Bradstreet* is the largest, they're also the most in demand and their cost is also the highest.

Right now just to obtain a DUN's number is going to be anywhere between $299 up to $699. It's only that high because *Dun and Bradstreet* know how important it is to setting up that process.

You'll also need to purchase the *DNBI Self Monitoring System*, which is a monthly system. The subscription is somewhere between $39 and $99 a month.

When you activate your DUN's number you get your file, a *Dun and Bradstreet* actual rating. The *Dun and Bradstreet* rating can also cost you anywhere between $299 and $899.

You can see there are definitely some fees involved with establishing those three credit bureaus, but through this process of doing it here on your own, you're going to want to go through there and set that up.

You need to know where you're at and be able to track that.

A business credit report can be started much the same as a consumer report commonly is with small credit cards. The business can be approved for small credit cards to help them build the initial credit profile.

Those types of initial cards in the business world are usually referred to as vendor credit. I think that's what we're going to talk about next.

GREG: Marco, I really appreciate you explaining the difference between those credit bureaus and some of the steps we need to take to see where our credit score is.

There are also some other terms and items businesses can use and now grow their credit score. I want to spend a few minutes talking about them.

The first one is going to be developing net 30, 60 and 90 terms. For some of the business owners who may be unfamiliar with these terms, what do you mean by this and what kind of an impact can setting up these terms have for your business?

MARCO: So, 30/60/90 term accounts are going to be the vendor accounts. A vendor line of credit is when a company or a vendor extends to you a line of credit to your business on these net 15/30/60/90 day terms.

What that means is you can purchase their produce or service up to a maximum amount. The net terms I just stated are essentially the time you're allowed to pay your bill in full.

If you have a net 15 account, you have 15 days to pay back whatever you borrowed. If you have a net 30, you have 30 days and so on.

That's going to be the time window they give you to pay that back. Paying it within those terms they set you up with you is extremely, extremely important.

One of the things I did not mention is that in comparison to consumer credit there are five factors that make up your credit score on the consumer side. They're things like what your balance is on your credit card, how many accounts you have open and how long the accounts been open.

On the business credit side there is only one component. That component is – do you pay your bill on time?

If you're paying it on time and doing it every month, the only thing that's going to happen is your score is going to go up. The scale is going to be 0-100.

So, if you have a 100 business credit score, you have the best possible.

The reality is that anything above an eighty is going to get you approved for pretty much anything. Anything below an eighty is going to get tough. And of course, as you go lower and lower you're going to be at a point where you're not going to be able to obtain business funding.

It's extremely important you pay those net terms back appropriately.

If you're set up on net 30 terms and you were to purchase $300 worth of good today, then that $300 is due within the next thirty days.

That in simple terms the way that process work.

You can get products and stuff for your business needs and defer the payments on the thirty days. What that does is pretty much eases your cash flow.

Some vendors will approve your company for net 30 payment terms upon verification of as little as having an *EIN* number, and a 4-1-1 listing.

Again, that goes back to module two and talking about how even those little steps are important.

Imagine applying and all you really have set up is your *EIN* and your 4-1-1 and you get approved for that. You're already starting the business credit building process.

There are just a couple of little things I do want to mention about the vendor accounts. You should always apply first without using your social, if possible. Some vendors will request it and some will tell you on the phone they need to have it, but you should still try and submit without it first.

When your first net 30 reports, your "trade line" to *Dun and Bradstreet*, the Dun system will automatically activate your file if it isn't already. That's also true for *Experian* and *Equifax*.

Those are important things to remember.

We do want to be honest about this. Some vendors do require an initial pre-pay order before they can approve your business for terms.

Just be prepared for that in some cases, not all but in some.

You need to have a total of at least five net 30 day pay accounts reporting. That's also very important.

Your vendors do not necessarily have to serve one hundred percent of your business needs. Keep that in mind as well.

Again, I have to reiterate this. Pay you net 30 vendor accounts in full and on time.

You must be patient with this process. You must allow time for the vendor recording cycles to get into the reporting system.

It usually takes three cycles of net account reports to build credit scores. You're looking at usually about a ninety-day process.

In most cases once you get started with vendor credit you're going to be looking at least ninety-days before you can get this whole business credit score set up and built if you don't have one already.

GREG: Marco, I love the way that you broke down how to use these net terms in our business.

To paint a picture and wrap our heads around this, I'd love it if you could maybe share an example or two of some businesses that are using terms in their business that can really have an impact on us.

MARCO: Absolutely.

One of the larger vendors that offer this kind of a service is going to be *Radio Shack*. Everybody knows who *Radio Shack* is.

I've talked to a lot of people that say, "I haven't been to a *Radio Shack* in a really long time." Obviously places like *Best Buy*, *Amazon* and these other types of things are where people go now to get most of their electronics and things.

Radio Shack still offers some real niche products that are unique to them, which is a big part of the reason they're still running right now.

They are one of the biggest credit vendors that are out there. They are probably the nation's most experience and trusted consumer electronic specialty retailer.

They provide computers, phones, batteries, cables and connectors. Sometimes people say, "What do I need to go to *Radio Shack* for? I really don't need anything from them."

What you have to understand is I'm not so much saying I want you to go to *Radio Shack* for the heck of it. The purpose is to buy something from this place so you can begin a business credit building process.

Who cares if it's a connector cable or some oddball wire you need, or it's batteries for crying out loud? It doesn't matter.

The point is to buy a little bit from there and pay it back. You will begin to build business credit. You using this as a tool is ultimately what it boils down to.

For instance, *Radio Shack* reports to both *Dun and Bradstreet* and *Experian*. They do not report to *Equifax*. That's why it's important to open up several different vendors.

That way you have some stuff going to this one and some going to the other. That way you'll be reporting to all three by the time you're done.

Radio Shack will put a business credit report to see how your business has paid bills in the past. If there isn't enough data on the business credit report they will ask you for bank and trade references.

Your business must be around for at least two years to get approved with *Radio Shack*. That's their particular criteria.

A *Dun and Bradstreet* number is required. Credit references are also required. You want to also make sure that is in place and set up.

Their payment terms are net 30. You will have thirty days to pay them back.

You can call *1-800-442-7221* to get an application. What you do is you fill it out and fax it back to them, like I talked about earlier. That's the way they handle this process. You send that to *(817)-415-3909* and fax it back to that number.

We'll put this information in the action in the action guide in the resources page so you can have that as well.

Another one I want to talk about is a service called *Quill.com*. They are an office supply vendor. They have office supplies, cleaning supplies, packing, shipping and school supplies, printing supplies, and all kinds of things.

They have a wide range of discounted top name brand products. They report to *Dun and Bradstreet*.

You must place your first order before you can be considered for a net 30 account. So, you buy something with the, set up a little bit of a relationship and then they'll consider you for a net 30 account.

If you have a *Dun and Bradstreet* score established, you will probably get approved with your initial order.

New businesses with little to no credit history will probably be put on a ninety-day pre payment schedule. If you make an order every month for ninety days they will more than likely approve you for a net 30 account.

That's why these guys are going to be great for the business credit building process.

New businesses can start out with smaller limits that will increase when they pay on time every month. These guys are net 30 processors.

Those are just two examples of two of the vendors out there. There are plenty more of them.

We're going to talk a little more about what else we offer for individuals who really want to get some assistance in this at the end of the program. But, as far as that process goes, you want to try and establish those on your own as much as possible.

We'll talk a little more about what else we offer to help where we can kind of hold your hand and get you set up with ever more of those with some assistance.

GREG: Marco, I really appreciate you sharing those examples with us on how to develop these net 30/60/90 terms with different vendors and the impact it can have on our business and business credit

In taking the next step in this evolution is creating what you call a revolving account.

I want you to explain to us what these revolving accounts are and then share an example with us of how we can begin to use this in our business.

MARCO: Absolutely, Greg.

Once you have established those vendor accounts through the net 30/60/90, the next step in the process is to start applying to actual revolving credit.

Revolving credit is pretty much going to be the final step in the process before you're able to go and apply for basic bank loans and those kinds of things.

I just want to give a couple quick examples. The first I want to talk about would be *Dell* computers.

We all know who *Dell* computers are. They actually report to *Dun and Bradstreet*. The cool thing about *Dell* is they will regularly approve small business automatically for $10,000 in business credit with a payment score of seventy-five or above with *Dun and Bradstreet*.

So, again, the scale with *Dun and Bradstreet* and the DUN's number, which is a paid 'x' number is zero through one hundred. If you've got at least a seventy-five or higher these guys are going to right away approve you for ten grand.

You shouldn't apply unless you've been in business for at least six months. They will check your personal credit in most cases. It is good to make sure where possible you can have the best possible personal credit.

That is something we can help you with as well. There'll be more information about that in the action guide.

To apply they require current employer names, social security number, birthday, mother's maiden name, identification numbers like driver's license and thing like that. That is obviously a revolving account like I said.

Just to give you a comparison, if you were to apply for a *Lowe's* account, *Lowe's* reports to *Dun and Bradstreet* and *Experian*.

You can apply online for an approval with a *Dun and Bradstreet* number. Most approvals are usually in the range of $1,000 to $5,000 right away.

They do require you be in business for at least three years. Otherwise, you're going to have to have a personal guarantor on the account unless you've got a really good *Dun and Bradstreet* or *Experian* score established.

Again, that's why it's so important to have that set up and ready to go. You can get approved in as little as forty-five seconds through an online application or they will mail you a letter.

I just wanted to go over a couple of those examples of how that revolving process and how important that is.

GREG: Marco, thank you for breaking that down for us and really getting us ready.

What I want to talk now is the fact that we've covered a lot of the action steps and the things we need to do in order to establish our credibility to begin building credit for our business.

I want to talk about the next step. Once we've got all these things in place it's time to go out and get the money, get the funding.

What is the next step in order to actually get the funding?

MARCO: The next step in the process is to make sure all these key components we've spoken about are in place. Once those items are in place you will be able to get access to funding. That's where you're going to be able to start applying.

Once you've gone through all this process here and you've established a high business credit score, the road is going to be very, very smooth from that point on.

If you don't put these items in place, you will encounter roadblock after roadblock.

That's a big part of the problem. In our experience we've seen that previously the business credit building process has been filled with roadblocks.

The information you received today, a lot of times just that information alone is extremely hard to come across. But, there are even more business credit building roadblocks that are usually out there.

We feel like we also have developed a powerful system to help business owners overcome that. So, some of the key business credit roadblocks we see and want to help you overcome are the fact that business credit does take time to build. Usually it's about four to six months.

Many times it's limited access to credit sources and mostly only store credit cards. Many times it has limited access to information about qualifying requirements of those credit sources.

You might ask, "What do I need to get approved for that particular type of account?" They don't even list that information half of the time.

Prior to our system there have been no certified business coaches available. And obviously it's difficult to get general access to funding.

We have a product we're offering now that is going to take this process we just covered and take it to the next level.

If you don't mind, Greg, I'd like to talk a little bit more about that and how we can help business owners overcome those roadblocks.

GREG: Yeah, Marco. I really think this is going to be a great resource for everyone that has taken the action steps you've laid out for them and now with what you and your team have been able to build, it bridges the gap to take everything they've created now to allow you and your system to get the funding for them.

So, go ahead and share it with everybody.

MARCO: This program we've written today with Brian Tracy is phenomenal. You're going to learn so many powerful things and be able to take this information, apply it and implement it immediately with your existing business or a business you hope to start.

Read every bit of this then re-read it again. It's powerful.

We also know there are a lot of steps involved and we know how busy you are as a business owner. We do have an additional program that's available for those who want to go ahead and get some assistance in this business credit building process.

This is our flagship product. It is our business-funding suite. I do just want to briefly talk about that for those who are interested in getting more assistance in this.

The business-funding suite is going to be the only place in the world where you're going to be able to have access to a certified business credit coach.

Essentially what's happening is you're going to enter into this program. You'll be given a login and a password.

You'll be going through this process very similarly to what we've talked about here in this book to make sure you have all the little foundation credibility steps taken care of first. It's going to help you make sure those are in place as well as give you additional resources if you don't already know where to go for that.

That's going to be the first step in the process. After that, you as part of our program will have access to a vast, vast network of potential lenders.

We have over 2,100 lenders in our system whom are ready and eager to lend to those who are part of our program. In addition to that, the certified business credit coach is going to handhold and walk you through this actual business funding establishment process.

They are essentially going to be the middleman between you and those 2,100 potential lenders out there. Their pay is going to be based upon their success and the service they provide you. As part of this program you will be overwhelmed with the service you're given as well as the opportunities that are available through this.

Like I've previously stated, prior to this it's been very difficult to even find out who's offering stuff and what the terms are. All of this information is laid out in the business-funding suite we are offering.

We're also going to be able to provide you with a free DUN's number, like I showed you earlier could cost you as much as $700 to $800. You're going to get access to that for free through this system.

You're also going to get something that's really awesome and one of a kind through this system as well. That is a real-time monitoring of your credit score, your business credit score.

On the consumer side this doesn't even exist. The technology is not even available, period. On the business side you will not find it anywhere outside of our program. It does not exist anywhere in the world, period.

This is the only place where the business bureaus have agreed to grant access in real time to the members of our program credit monitoring so they can see exactly what's happening to their credit score as it's happening.

That is a very powerful tool.

If you are interested in more information about this, please review the action guide. We'll have the links there where you'll be able to see exactly how this process works.

We'll have more resources available to you if you want to dive a little bit deeper into this.

It is powerful and it will allow you to take things to the next level. Best of all, we offer a $50,000 guarantee in this program. You will obtain at least $50,000 in non-personally guaranteed business financing regardless of your personal credit, regardless of those types of issues like that as part of this program.

It is amazing and it's powerful.

GREG: Marco, this is an amazing resource for any small business that is ready to take the lead in their business and see the success they want to see for themselves.

I know we started in module one by talking about your story and some of the hardships and mountains you had to overcome in order to begin starting your own business.

Now you have the opportunity to help others take that next step in their business. I've never seen anything like this program before. I think it's a great opportunity for business owners to take that next step to get that business funding that's going to take their business to the heights they really want to see for themselves. Marco, what's the next step? How can they get in touch with you and begin working with you in this program?

MARCO: I appreciate everything you've mentioned, Greg. You're exactly right.

I've had to walk down some of those valleys and trenches. I've had to go through some real painful things, but it's made me who I am today. I think a lot of the potential business owner listening and reading this are going to be able to connect with that.

It is challenging and it's not easy, but again, we have to remind ourselves where we are. We're in the United States of America. This is the place to be for the small business owner.

If you have even a little bit of a calling for that, I really would emphasize to just get out there, follow your dream and do it. Especially don't let funding issues hold you back.

We do have one of our programs in our system, which is specifically designed for startups. It offers up to $150,000 for a brand new business. Personal credit is definitely a big factor on that, but it is available for those who are wanting to launch something.

There are a lot of different programs and resources. Don't let anything get in your way. Don't let anybody get in your way. If there are naysayers in your life, you're going to have to find a way to silence them and follow you dream.

If we can be of assistance to you in any way then please give us a call. The phone number to reach us is *1-888-900-5138* if you'd like to talk more about the actual business-funding suite.

We'll have some websites you can visit. I've got some videos and things available, which we're going to talk a little bit more about the actual program itself.

Don't forget to implement what you learned in this book. It is powerful stuff and it will work. But, if you do need some assistance, some more hand holding and the 50K guarantee, call us and we'll talk more about the price and how long it takes and the details of all that. We want to help you take things to the next level.

GREG: I truly believe you do want to help all these business. I can hear the passion and fire in your voice as you begin talking about helping these small businesses out.

I encourage everyone to start by going through your action. Go through all the steps, actions and resources that Marco and Brian Tracy have laid out for you to begin taking the next step in your business growth.

When you are ready to take advantage of the program Marco has put together for you, I encourage you to give him a call today at *1-888-900-5138* to see how Marco can really help your business.

Marco, I really do want to thank you and Brian Tracy for sharing this wealth of information. I know it's going to be a game changer for the businesses that not just consume it, but to actually take action and implement these steps into their business. Thank you again for spending some time with us and helping small businesses today.

MARCO: It's my pleasure. Greg, thank you.

GREG: One again, please go through your action guide, take action and we look forward to seeing the success of your business. We'll talk soon.

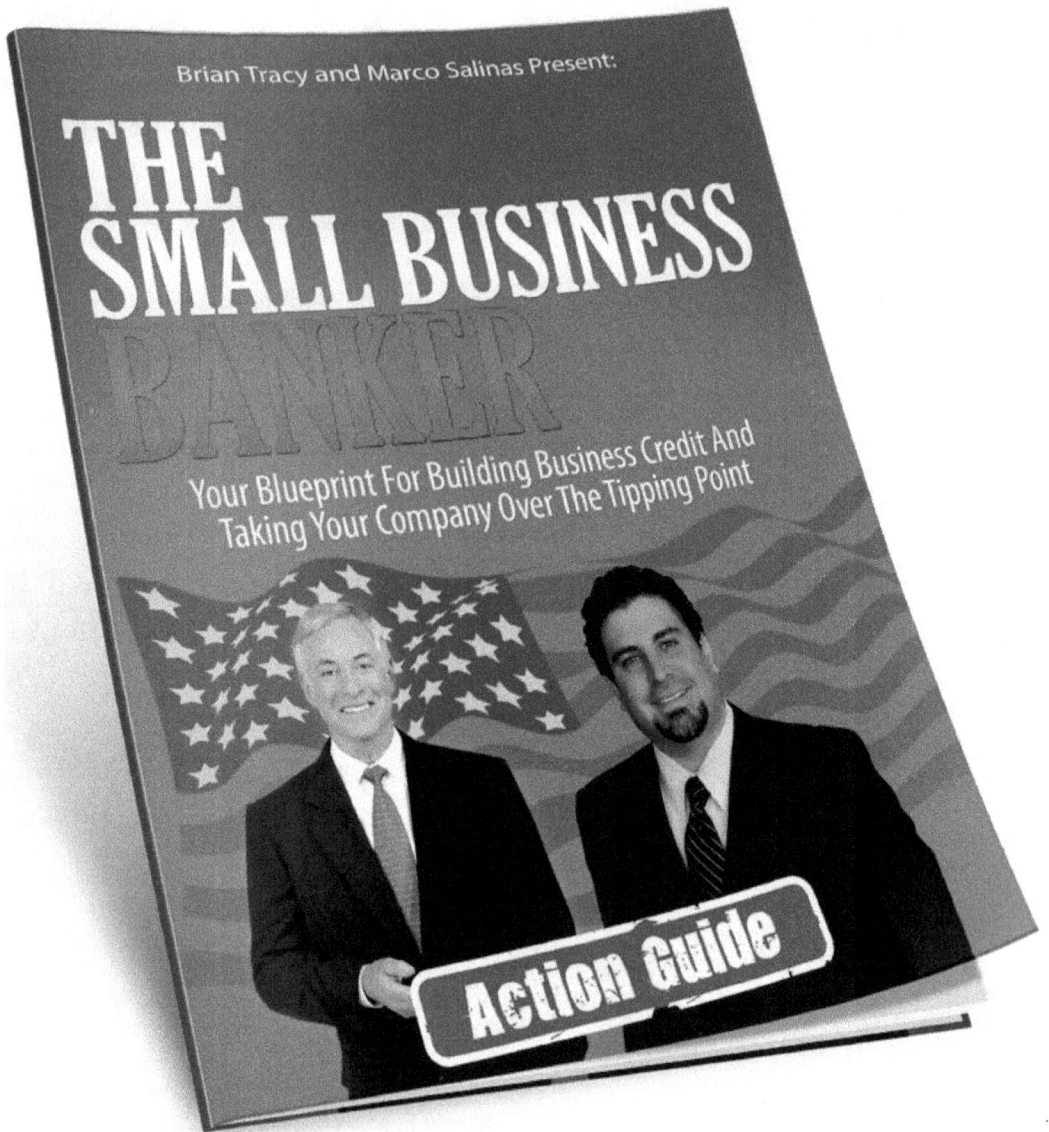

The Small Business Banker
Action Guide

Featuring
Brian Tracy & Marco Salinas

Module 1: What A Successful Business Looks Like Today

Measure Your Success:

Rate your business on a scale of 1 to 5 in the following areas, 5 being excellent and 1 being poor.

Customer Service:

1   2   3   4   5

Customer Feedback:

1   2   3   4   5

Word-of-mouth Advertisement:

1   2   3   4   5

Customer Satisfaction:

1   2   3   4   5

Consistently Returning Customers:

1   2   3   4   5

Which areas did you rate yourself lowest? Why do you believe these are problem areas for you?

_____

_____

_____

_____

What is the foundation of business and how do you measure the business' success?

_____

_____

_____

_____

Utilize Zero-Based Thinking:

What is Zero-Based Thinking?

_____

_____

_____

Is there any product or service your business offers that you would not have brought to the market, knowing what you know now? Which products or services are they and why would you not offer them?

_____

_____

_____

_____

What would you offer as an alternative?

_____

_____

_____

_____

Are there any processes or expenditures in your business that would not have used knowing what you know now? What are they and why would you not use them?

_____

_____

_____

_____

_____

What would you do in place of those processes or expenditures?

_____

_____

_____

_____

_____

Are there people you have hired or are working with that, knowing what you know now, you would not have hired? Who are they and why would you not have hired or worked with them?

_____

_____

_____

_____

What would you do to prevent hiring or working alongside people like the ones you mentioned? How would you prevent the problems you encountered with them?

_____

_____

_____

_____

_____

Create Goals:

What does your product offer to your customers?

_____

_____

_____

What do you hope to accomplish through offering your product?

_____

_____

_____

Where would you like to see your business in:

One Month:

_____

_____

_____

Six Months:

_____

_____

_____

Twelve Months:

_____

_____

_____

Two years:

_____

_____

_____

Ten Years:

_____

_____

_____

Build The Right Team:

Explain the law of three that should be used for hiring new employees.

_____

_____

Who are three people you would trust to help interview a potential employee?

1.

2.

3.

Why is it important to make sure your team has clarity about your business and purpose?

_____

_____

Analyze Your Product:

How does Brian suggest that you organize at your varied products and services?

_____

_____

Try this process with your products. Divide your products into categories and choose one category for the following exercise. Repeat this process with your other categories of products as well.

What is the main product you sell in this category?

_____

_____

Knowing what you know now, would you still have offered this product to the market?

_____

_____

Do you believe this product works? What are it's benefits? List at least 5 benefits.

1.

2.

3.

4.

5.

Narrow those benefits down to one. What is the primary benefit customers can expect from this product or service?

_____

_____

Action Steps:
- If you answered that you wouldn't bring your product to the market knowing what you now know, discontinue that product.
- If you couldn't come up with 5 benefits for your product, rethink the product. How can you make it better, faster, cheaper or easier to use? Analyze all your products this way.

Module 2: Marketing And Branding Your Business

Identify Your Customers

What are the four pressing needs your products and services should satisfy?

1.

2.

3.

4.

Do your products and services provide for these needs? If so, where are your customers? Who are they? Use the space below to brainstorm and begin narrowing your customer base.

_____

_____

_____

_____

What are the four parts to marketing strategy you should think about?

1.

2.

3.

4.

What are the 7 parts of the marketing mix?

1.

2.

3.

4.

5.

6.

7.

Who do you think is your ideal customer? Use the space below to identify specific characteristics of your ideal customer.

Age:

_____

Income:

_____

Educational Background:

_____

Level of Family Formation:

_____

Occupation:

_____

Fears, wants and needs:

_____

_____

Hopes and aspirations:

_____

_____

What moves or motivates them?

_____

_____

Where do they buy? What value do they seek?

_____

_____

What media sells effectively to this type of customer?

_____

_____

How can you benefit from a strategic alliance?

_____

_____

_____

Additional Notes:

_____

_____

_____

_____

Action Step:
- Make contact with your customers! Now that you know who your customer is, be in constant connection with them. Learn how to market to them. Grab their attention.

Module 3: Building An Everlasting Business

Survive Tough Economies:

What is the key to the success of your business?

_____

_____

What product or service did you begin your business to revolve around?

_____

_____

Is that product or service still your most valuable offering? Why or why not?

_____

_____

_____

What extensions have you made since your business' beginning that may not be doing as well as your original product or service?

_____

_____

_____

_____

Do you keep in contact with old customers to keep them returning for more business? How can you take advantage of old customers to bring in new business? Brainstorm below:

_____

_____

_____

_____

Why is it important to get control over your debt?

_____

_____

_____

Additional Notes:

_____

_____

_____

_____

Action Steps:
- If you have extensions beyond your original product or service that aren't successful, cut them from your business immediately.
- Focus on connecting with your customers, old and new. Find ways to reconnect with customers who haven't recently returned to your business.

Module 4: Separating You From Your Business

Use the space below to mark the differences between personal credit and business credit. Include your personal notes as well.

Personal Credit	Business Credit

How will you and your business benefit from establishing its own line of credit?

_____

_____

_____

_____

What is the best way to establish your business's own line of credit?

_____

_____

_____

_____

The 5 Reasons Why Your Business Needs to Build A Business Credit Asset:

#1 Access to funding and managing cash flow is the single biggest concern for business owners.
By establishing and building a Business Credit Asset™, businesses can access new funding sources to ensure positive cash flow.

#2 Secure new financing options
A strong business credit file can be the difference between receiving funds or not. Approval for most small business loan decisions under $90,000 happens automatically, often relying on one thing - your business credit file and score.

#3 Get the best credit terms
Your business credit score will likely result in better credit card and loan interest rates. For businesses with weak credit scores, banks and lending institutions may increase loan interest rates from 7% to 12% and credit card interest rates from 8% to 18%.

#4 Reduce your expenses
Building a business Credit Asset can improve cash flow by reducing:

- Financing Costs
- Insurance Premiums
- Rental Terms
- Credit Card Rates
- Vendor and Supplier Terms

#5 Peace of mind
Protect your personal assets and reduce your personal liability by creating a separate corporate entity and business credit. Establishing your business credit asset only strengthens this liability protection.

Action steps to help you form a corporation or LLC:

✓ Visit www.BusinessCreditTools.com.

✓ Take advantage of the assistance provided on the site.

✓ Visit your local bookstore and research small business books for your field.

✓ Commit to fully educating yourself.

✓ Decide which kind of business entity is best for you` to form.

Module 5: Business Credibility Building Process

Why is business credibility an essential step in obtaining business credit, funding and financing?

_____

_____

_____

Key Components For Building Credibility

Use the following pages as an opportunity to take notes on the 13 key components to exceed lender credibility standards. Then work through the checklist, checking each item until you've completed each step of the process.

Key #1: Business Name

_____

_____

_____

Key #2: Corporate Identity

_____

_____

_____

Key #3: EIN Number

_____

_____

_____

Key #4: Physical Address

_____

_____

_____

Key #5: 4-1-1 + 1-800 Phone Listings + Fax Machine

_____

_____

_____

Key #6: Website Address

_____

_____

_____

Key #7: Email Address

_____

_____

_____

Key #8: Licensing

_____

_____

_____

Key #9: Bank Account

_____

_____

_____

Key #10: Business Listings

_____

_____

_____

Key #11: Taxes and Tax Returns

_____

_____

_____

Key #12: Property Liens and Judgements

_____

_____

_____

Key #13: Business Model

_____

_____

_____

Key Component Checklist:

- ☐ Business Name

- ☐ Corporate Identity

- ☐ EIN Number

- ☐ Physical Address

- ☐ 4-1-1 + 1-800 Phone Listings + Fax Machine

- ☐ Website Address

- ☐ Email Address

- ☐ Licensing

- ☐ Bank Account

- ☐ Business Listings

- ☐ Taxes & Tax Returns

- ☐ Property Liens & Judgements

- ☐ Business Model

Action Step:
- Work through the key components until you've marked each item on this list.

Module 6: The Business Credit System

Who are the three credit bureaus for consumer credit?

1.

2.

3.

Who are the three credit bureaus for business credit?

1.

2.

3.

Why is it important to get a copy of your business credit report?

_____

_____

_____

_____

What is a 30/60/90 term account and how can it benefit your business?

_____

_____

_____

_____

Steps To Obtaining Your Business Credit Report:

Experian
Website: www.SmartBusinessReports.com

Cost: $49-99

What You Get: Find out how many trade lines you have reporting, see if you have business credit lines set up, verify if you have an active *Experian* business profile in place, update on recent inquiries and *Experian* credit score.

Equifax
Website: www.Equifax.com/Small-Business/Credit-Report/ensb

Cost: $99.95

What You Get: Full Credit Report

Dun & Bradstreet
Website: www.DNB.com

Cost: $299-699

What You Get: Helps enable your business to borrow without a personal guarantor. You will get your file as well as your *Dun & Bradstreet* Rating.

Additional Costs:
Monthly subscription to DNBI Self Monitoring System: $39-69/month

Dun and Bradstreet Rating comes at an additional cost: $299-899

Vendor Examples

Radio Shack:

About: Offer niche products, unique to their store for electronic resources such as cables, connectors, batteries, phones and computers.

Report To: Both Dun & Bradstreet and Experian.

Criteria: Your business needs to have been established for at least two years to qualify for an account.

Payment Terms: Net 30

Contact:
   To Request Application:1-800-442-7221
   To Fax Application: 817-415-3909

Quill.com

About: Provide office supplies, cleaning supplies, packing, shipping, printing and school supplies.

Report To: Dun & Bradstreet.

Criteria: You must place your first order before you can open an account.

Payment Terms: For new businesses, you may be put on a 90-day prepayment schedule. Once approved, they offer Net 30 accounts.

Important Tips For Establishing 30/60/90 Term Accounts:

- Try to apply without using your social security number.

- Prepare for a possible initial pre-pay before setting up your account with some vendors.

- Always pay accounts in full and on time

- It usually takes 3 cycles of reports to update your credit score. (90 day process)

- You have no obligation to your vendors; they do not have to serve one hundred percent of your business needs.

Business Credit Builder Program™

$50,000 Guarantee

How would you like to know, with absolute certainty, that you are making the best decision in choosing a partner to build your business credit?

Well, Now You Can. We Offer an Unmatched $50,000 Guarantee!

We understand that building a Business Credit Asset™ is serious, it takes time and dedication on your part and we want to make you certain that choosing us as a partner is the absolute best decision you could make to help you establish your business credit.

How Do We Ensure Your Success?

Simple…we have experienced Certified Business Credit Coaches that will guide you, step-by-step through the Credit Building Development Process™. We are there for you 100% of the time. You will have access to an interactive Business Credit Development Platform that will keep track of your progress and give you guidance on your next steps. The interactive Business Credit Development Platform, coupled with the help of your Certified Business Credit Coach is a sure fire way to achieve business credit results.

What Is Our Guarantee?

We want to make sure you are successful in your pursuit of business credit and financing options. While there are many things we can control, there are some things we cannot control. For example, we cannot control how soon you will be approved for financing. That will depend on the specifics of you and your business. The good news is that we can control many other aspect of the business credit-coaching program. Here is what we can control and what we guarantee:

- Corporate Compliance and documentation review

- Discount on D&B file and a D&B rating

- D&B Paydex Score

- Business credit file with Corporate Experian with an intelliscore

- Business credit file with business Equifax with the appropriate business credit score.

- Trade accounts and/or Vendor Accounts with and without a personal guarantee.

- A Business Credit Asset™ that can be used to leverage financing opportunities

- Access to a dedicated funding advisor

- $50,000 GUARANTEE: we will continue to work with you UNTIL you have been extended up to $50,000 in business credit.

In other words, we are so confident in our system that if after the initial 6 months of following our program, you will be extended up to $50,000 in business credit or we will continue to coach you, at NO COST, until you do!

See how our Business Credit Coaching and Funding Consultation Services stack up with the competition:

Benefits:	Credit 360 Business Funding	Other Companies
Largest Database of Business Lenders	✓	✗
Data Integration of Over 100 Different Cash Business Lenders	✓	✗
Data Integration of D & B	✓	✗
Data Integration of Experian	✓	✗
Data Integration of Equifax	✓	✗
Discount D & B File	✓	✗
Certified Coaches	✓	✗
One-On-One Coaching	✓	*Some*
Coaches' Pay Tied to Client Success	✓	✗
Coaches' Pay Tied To Client Satisfaction	✓	✗

For more information about Marco Salinas or his 360 Business Funding Suite, visit www.BusinessCreditTools.com.

www.ingramcontent.com/pod-product-compliance
Lightning Source LLC
Chambersburg PA
CBHW062027210326
41519CB00060B/7191